Praying
Through

To Paul,
The Lord Bless you
and keep you
with love, Gwen xx

Praying Through

FINDING WHOLENESS AND HEALING IN THE PRAYERS OF DAVID

JOHN KITCHEN

CLC
PUBLICATIONS

Fort Washington, PA 19034

Published by CLC ❖ Publications

U.S.A.
P.O. Box 1449, Fort Washington, PA 19034

GREAT BRITAIN
51 The Dean, Alresford, Hants. SO24 9BJ

AUSTRALIA
P.O. Box 2299, Strathpine, QLD 4500

NEW ZEALAND
10 MacArthur Street, Feilding

ISBN 978-0-87508-978-2

Contents

To
Julie

my
"sweet psalmist"

Prologue

THROUGH. Not *to*. Not *into*. Not *around*. Not toward, over, under or against. *Through!* We must pray through. Life must be prayed through as a whole—an unbroken, life-long thread of communion with God. Life also must be prayed through one episode at a time—wringing from it every opportunity for intimacy with God. It is not that we don't pray—we pray *about* our concerns, *over* worrisome matters, *before* big events, *in* distress, *for* our wishes, *under* stress, *concerning* troubles, *around* the issues, *toward* a desired end and *against* feared outcomes—but too often we don't pray *through*.

Praying through is not a quick-fix remedy, not a speedy escape from life's pain. There is no assured formula to praying through, guaranteeing that at a fixed point the pain will lessen. We don't pray through for just five minutes, five days or five months; there can be no fixed timetable to a breakthrough to the other side. But there is the guarantee that God is there all the while and that there is a breakthrough into His life. There is another side. There is another life, God's divine life, that He is extending to us, longing for us to enter into. Praying through is not one more treatment, method or option to be tried and weighed for its suitability for our needs. Praying through is the divinely ordained narrow road to life, a shared life, God's life as your life.

But what does that mean? What does that look like? How would that sound? What would be said? Must *anything* be said? Our questions are answered, our ears tuned, our eyes enlightened when we turn to the book of Psalms.

The Psalms, however, are not simply a book. They are no mere collection of poems but a compilation of life—all of it, the highs and the lows, the ecstasies and the agonies, the invocations and the imprecations, the praises and the screaming doubts. This is precisely why we need the Psalms. They are *life*. They are for *all* of life—*my* life, *your* life. As Kathleen Norris has noted, "In these poems of Scripture, you'll find rage, loneliness and fear—in other words, you'll find yourself."[1]

> *It is not that we don't pray, but too often we don't pray through. Praying through is not a quick-fix remedy for life's pain; it is the divinely ordained narrow road to life—God's life as your life.*

As the psalmists' words become our words to God, we find ourselves praying through the problems of life. Athanasius long ago noted that as we pray the psalms they "become like a mirror to the person singing them."[2]

The psalms were prayers set to music. The ancient Israelites apparently had no system of musical notation or score, or at least none that has survived. But what remains is the throbbing intensity of the cries, imprecations, lamentations, praises and prayers of souls just like ours. The fourteen psalms before us are those psalms of David whose titles bear some historical footnote as to the time and circumstances of their composition.[3] As we trace them chronologically,[4] we find ourselves praying through life— through David's, through ours—and most importantly, into God's. Here we find life not merely as we wish it to be, but as it is and, if we are willing, as God will make it to be.

I invite you, then, to come journey through David's life. We'll travel not merely the trails of history and fact, but of a heart praying through the passages of earthly life and emerging into the divine life God offers us.

Should we choose to live in the Psalms, our souls will find their voice. We will discover that in the midst of life's flow we speak, God hears and, even if nothing appears to have changed, everything will be different.

1

Praying Through Betrayal

A NERVOUS puff of breath enveloped the flame dancing above the oil lamp, extinguishing it and blanketing the room in darkness. In the still blackness two huddled forms struggled to silence their breathing and wrestle their fears into submission. Silently David raised himself along the wall toward the second floor window. As he slipped himself behind the curtain and leveled his eyes over the sill, he whispered just loud enough for his wife to hear, "They're out there." He couldn't see them, but he knew his words were true.

He slowly turned his back to the wall and slumped to the floor in dejected confusion. His wife crawled across the floor to join him. They sat in silence for several minutes, staring together at some indefinite point in the darkness.

Finally she broke the trance. "What happened?"

Moments before she had been quietly tending to household chores when the door had flown open and her husband screamed "Get down!" as he plunged them into blinding darkness. The only words that came to David's lips were, "Your father . . ." Enough said. Michal knew exactly what he meant.

More silence. More staring. Finally she asked, "Another spear?"

"Yes," he blankly replied.

"Why?"

"Why did he do it the first time? Who knows. It's the evil spirit, I guess."

Michal broke another extended silence by asking, "What now?"

There came no answer. There was not one to give. At least not one worth using a breath to explain. They both saved their breath, but their minds were working overtime: *Why would her father the king want to kill his most loyal subject, faithful warrior and son-in-law?*

They both jolted to full attention as a sound at the bottom of the stairs shattered their stupor. Shaking herself out of her confusion, Michal took her husband's head in her hands and, with nose nearly touching nose, she said in as emphatic a voice as he'd ever heard her use, "If you don't escape with your life tonight, tomorrow you'll be killed."

David knew she was right. The soldiers could be heard collecting themselves on the floor below. Groping through the darkness, Michal grabbed up every loose piece of cloth she could find. She knotted one piece to another until she had a suitable length of rope. David tied it off inside the room and lept to the window. He paused, turned and took his wife in his arms. Neither knew how long that embrace would have to last. He felt her hair, kissed her lips and whispered his love to her.

In a flash David was back at the window and down the rope. Michal peered out the window and watched her husband streak for cover in the nearby trees.[1]

• • • • •

It would take some doing to stab yourself in the back. It's a maneuver that normally requires assistance. You must first trust your back to another. That is a move we manage to pull off repeatedly, despite a truckload of experience warning us of the danger. Naivetè might be what lulls us into vulnerability in the beginning, but down the road it's that inner, irrepressible longing for relationship. Even with a string of bad experiences behind us, we just keep coming back to this thing called relationship.

Giving the gift of trust almost unavoidably leads to receiving the curse of betrayal at some point. Not everyone we trust turns on us—it only feels that way. That predictable percentage point of pain, though comparatively small, too often dominates our thinking. In fact the all-pervasive pain of betrayal makes us reluctant even to pray. Prayer and trust are two inseparable strata of the same substance. Praying is, in a sense, trusting your back to God. Intellectually most of us know God won't betray us, but the throbbing ache of yesterday's relationships makes us hesitate to find out.

Prayer and trust are inseparable. Praying is, in a sense, trusting your back to God.

By its nature pain distorts our perceptions—thus the expression "blinding pain." It points to a pain so acute that all else is pushed to the background. Intensify the anguish enough and life itself becomes less valuable than simply ending the pain. It's what makes otherwise stable people consider suicide. Pain is powerful, and there is no relational pain quite as piercing as betrayal. It distorts reality, and in so doing it threatens our ability to pray.

Psalm 59 lays bare our struggle to shake off the distortions brought on by the pain of betrayal. Throughout the psalm David wrestles with reality and refuses to let it go. Isn't that what we all struggle in prayer to do?

Psalm 59

To the choirmaster: according to Do Not Destroy. A Miktam of David, when Saul sent men to watch his house in order to kill him.

¹ Deliver me from my enemies, O my God;
protect me from those who rise up against me;
² deliver me from those who work evil,
and save me from bloodthirsty men.

Clarity About God

Betrayal threatens to distort our view of God. God doesn't look the same through tears as through triumph. He *is* the same; it's just our perception that has changed. Our circumstances act like a lens through which all the world, even God, is viewed. A number of these distortions are evident as David lifts this prayer from the cover of darkness. As Saul's men watched for David and as David watched for them, he lifted his prayer to God.

The dark night of betrayal plays tricks on the eyes of one's heart. Sometimes it makes us believe that God is inactive. David's prayer opens with a series of abrupt, hasty imperatives: "Deliver me . . . protect me . . . deliver me . . . save me" (vv. 1–2). David sounds like an ER doctor barking out orders to the medical staff around him as they fight for the life of the one lying before them, but this time the life is David's own. There is no one at his disposal but

God, and in the darkness David isn't so sure even about Him. There was no time to quibble or question—"God I need action, and I need it now!"

> *³For behold, they lie in wait for my life;*
> *fierce men stir up strife against me.*
> *For no transgression or sin of mine, O Lord,*
> *⁴for no fault of mine, they run and make ready.*
> *Awake, come to meet me, and see!*
> *⁵You, Lord God of hosts, are God of Israel.*
> *Rouse yourself to punish all the nations;*
> *spare none of those who treacherously plot evil. Selah*

Sometimes the pain of betrayal makes us think God is blind. David commanded God to "behold" (v. 3) and he ordered him to "see" (v. 4). Ever had the sense that God must be either blind or distracted? Reality, or at least my perception of it, seems so obvious to me. Why can't God see it?

Betrayal's stab sometimes leads us to believe that God is asleep.² David cried out to God, "Awake" (v. 4) and exhorted Him, "Rouse yourself" (v. 5). Think of it: the thing David was being deprived of as he hid from Saul's men, and the thing Saul's men were depriving themselves of as they searched for David—sleep—was the very thing he accuses God of indulging in! David was saying, in essence, "God, the only one getting any sleep around here is You!"

God is not inactive, nor is He blind or asleep. We *know* that. But we don't always *feel* that. When you've been betrayed by others the pain can be so acute that it threatens to obscure even what you know about God. Prayer is an act of the will in which, despite the pain, we lay hold again of that which we know to be reality. It may not feel like reality, but by faith we assert that it is. In prayer we doggedly refuse to let go of what we know despite all the arguments of our feelings.

> *8 But you, O Lord, laugh at them;*
>   *you hold all the nations in derision.*
> *9 O my Strength, I will watch for you,*
>   *for you, O God, are my fortress.*
> *10 My God in his steadfast love will meet me;*
>   *God will let me look in triumph on my enemies.*

Praying through betrayal is choosing to lay hold of God's perspective and refusing to accept any other version of reality. When we look at life through our pain, the facts appear so clear: God has forgotten me; He is blind to my plight; He is unaware of the tragedy that has befallen me. But praying through requires shaking off such phantom-realities. It is a resolute determination to see what God sees. That is what David was doing when he shook off his own perceptions and cried, "I will watch for you" (v. 9).

Praying through requires shaking off phantom-realities. It is a resolute determination to see what God sees.

Significantly, the word here translated "watch" is the same one we find in the psalm title describing the surveillance of Saul's men over David's home. What Saul's men did toward David, David was doing toward God. Watching for God is a spiritual discipline—a discipline that requires acting in opposition to what we *feel* is true so that we can embrace what *is* true. Discipline in prayer is choosing to act in accord with what we *know* to be true. Unfortunately in our world, truth is considered a glandular condition. Feelings are the ultimate truth. To think, act or choose contrary to current emotion is to be false, fake, inauthentic. This is the greatest sin of our secular culture. The child of God recognizes this seductive attitude, and fights it off in prayer, refusing to let go of objective truth.

The verb David uses with his next breath has the sense of "being in front of."[3] Thus when David says, "My God . . . will meet me" (v. 10), it means that he has set his eyes on the mist-enshrouded horizon of his personal experience and is watching for God to break through the haze and show Himself. It's as though David gritted his teeth and reminded himself, "My God is not preoccupied, blind or asleep. My God is before me. I may be distracted at the moment, but He is not at any moment. He has gone before me. As I continue forward in faith, He will meet me!"

Listen as David deals with the deceptions that betrayal sets before him. He voices who God is. Unfortunately the ESV does not include the word "But" that begins verse 5; thus we miss the emphatic nature of the pronoun: "[But] *You*, LORD God of hosts, are . . ."[4] "But" becomes a turning point in the psalm, so that from verse 5 on God is set in contrast to all of David's troubles and the distortions that they bring (vv. 1–4). The answer to all the confusion about God's whereabouts, character and activity is to remember who He indeed is.

He is the "LORD God of hosts." The word "*LORD*" is the covenant name Yahweh. It points to God's self-existence and faithfulness. As "God of hosts" He is the God of armies, both Israel's (who were, humanly speaking, under Saul's command) and of the angelic hosts of heaven. Imagine how rich this name for God must have been to David the warrior. This meant that those lying in wait for him were not ultimately Saul's army, or even David's future army. They were God's. He was their Commander-in-Chief. This battle did not pit David against Saul, but God's army against all who dared to stand in opposition to His child. As David lay breathless in the dark, he began to realize that he was not so much surrounded by Saul's men, but by God's angels. Elisha would later pray that God would open his servant's eyes to see, not the horsemen and chariots of Aram that had encircled the city, but the angelic hosts in their chariots of fire that had surrounded the army of Aram (2 Kings 6:17). So too David's eyes were opened in the darkness to see God as "the LORD God of hosts."

David also noted that he was under the care of "the God of Israel" (v. 5). Israel was God's nation, not Saul's. It was God's kingdom, not David's. God owned the nation that Saul was clinging to and which David had been anointed to lead.

> ¹¹*Kill them not, lest my people forget;*
> > *make them totter by your power and bring them down,*
> > *O Lord, our shield!*
> ¹²*For the sin of their mouths, the words of their lips,*
> > *let them be trapped in their pride.*
> *For the cursing and lies that they utter,*
> > ¹³*consume them in wrath;*
> > *consume them till they are no more,*
> *that they may know that God rules over Jacob*
> > *to the ends of the earth. Selah*

• • • • •

¹⁶But I will sing of your strength;
I will sing aloud of your steadfast love in the morning.
For you have been to me a fortress
and a refuge in the day of my distress.
¹⁷O my Strength, I will sing praises to you,
for you, O God, are my fortress,
the God who shows me steadfast love.

Listen to David's stubborn refusal to allow the pain of Saul's betrayal to blind him to the reality of who God is: "O my Strength . . . you, O God, are my fortress . . . O Lord, our shield . . . O my Strength . . . you, O God, are my fortress, the God who shows me steadfast love" (vv. 9, 11, 17). If you listen closely you'll detect the shift after verse 4 from panic to praise. Worship dispels the warped image of God that betrayal tries to sell us. The pain of betrayal threatens to distort my view of God, but the spiritual discipline of worship restores a clear view of who He really is.

Clarity About Circumstances

Pain, however, threatens to distort more than simply my view of God; it also threatens my view of circumstances. When David prayed, "Protect me from those who rise up against me" (v. 1), he was revealing his natural view of the facts. The word translated "protect" means to set up high on an inaccessible place. It is a remedy for one feeling vulnerable. Surrounded by Saul's men, unable to detect them in the night, not certain which tree they lurked behind— David had no idea from which direction they might launch their attack. He wanted God to pluck him up out of the midst of that mess and set him on high where he could look down upon those seeking his life. It was out of similar desperation that Meister Eckhart prayed, "What is this darkness? What is its name? Call it an aptitude for sensitivity. Call it a rich sensitivity which will make you whole. Call it your potential for vulnerability."

For David the "potential for vulnerability" was now a potential realized. Out of that position of vulnerability, David exercised his faith and asserted in prayer two facts about God. First, "you, O God, are my fortress" (vv. 9, 17). David could assert this as a present fact because it had been his past experience: "you have been to me a fortress and a refuge in the day of my distress" (v. 16). The pain of betrayal and the fear of all its threatened destruction can obscure the record of God's past faithfulness. By prayer we refuse to let go of who God has been and who He continues to be. Interestingly, the root of the word translated "fortress" (vv. 9, 17) is the same as the one translated "protect" (v. 1). What David needs God to be in the present is the very thing He has proven to be in the past. Faith measures current circumstances by the ruler of God's past faithfulness.

> *The pain of betrayal can obscure the record of God's past faithfulness. By prayer we refuse to let go of who God has been and who He continues to be.*

Second, David reasserted that "God rules over Jacob" (v. 13). God is both my fortress and my King. It was God who ruled over the nation of Israel—not Saul. David was not seduced even by the legitimate promise of his rule over the nation. Saul was not the ultimate king; neither was David. God alone is King! All authority and power lie with Him. There is no other king within, and there is no other kingdom without (see v. 8) that can threaten or disrupt the sovereign will of God.

Betrayal distorts my view of my circumstances, but the spiritual discipline of confident prayer rests me again on the rock of God's sovereign control.

Clarity About Tomorrow

The distortions brought on by the pain of betrayal are not confined, however, to our perception of God and our circumstances. Our view of the future can also be affected. Painful circumstances have an especially distorting effect upon the eyes of our hearts. Later Paul would pray for the believers in Ephesus that "the eyes of your heart may be enlightened, so that you may know what is the hope of His calling" (Eph. 1:18, NASB). Hope withers when present circumstances obscure the light of truth from our hearts.

As David breathlessly waited out Saul's men in the darkness, his hope began to grow weak. Too often "now" is all that seems certain. In verse 6 David pictured his pursuers as dogs sniffing through the darkness, howling and prowling. Verse 14 repeats and expands on this image, as a refrain of hopelessness comes to the surface of David's desperate cry:

> *⁶ Each evening they come back,*
> *howling like dogs*
> *and prowling about the city.*
> *⁷ There they are, bellowing with their mouths*
> *with swords in their lips—*

for "Who," they think, "will hear us?"

•   •   •   •   •

¹⁴ Each evening they come back,
    howling like dogs
    and prowling about the city.
¹⁵ They wander about for food
    and growl if they do not get their fill.

"Each evening they come back"—in pain, it seems the
"evening" is all there is. The moment, this second, my
current breath is all that is guaranteed me. Darkness and
night dominate. There is no hope of sunrise. There is no
anticipation of a new day. The present is all that is, with
no hope for anything beyond the immediate.

How well I remember the night many years ago when
a pack of wild dogs roamed through our area. In the dark
they found the helpless goats our landlord kept in a small
pasture next to our home. The manic howling, ravenous
barking and incessant bawl of the dogs filled the night,
lingering well into the early morning hours. I lay in the
dark feeling feeble and powerless to help. When I awoke,
the air was still. I raced to the window, looking out over
the pasture to the west. The lifeless, already bloating body
of a goat bobbed pathetically in the middle of the pond.
Drowning had seemed a lesser evil than the merciless teeth
of the dogs-of-the-night.

Those shrieks and that scene fill my mind as I hear David
describe Saul's men. Hearing their approach he felt utterly alone, powerless, helpless, abandoned. The sands of
his hour glass were slipping away. His predators were circling and moving in for the kill.

Despite his circunstances, David reached out in prayer and laid hold again of hope. Fixing his grip firmly on God's promise of tomorrow, he refused to let hope escape. He reminded himself and God that there were standing promises that guaranteed "the morning" and with it a fresh experience of God's "steadfast love" (v. 16).

We've already noted the repeated refrain of despair (vv. 6–7, 14–15), but something different follows each one. In the face of despair David first asserted, "But you, O Lord, laugh at them" and then later "But I will sing of your strength" (vv. 8, 16). God's laughter is a picture of the chuckle of sovereignty in the face of presumption (see Ps. 2:1–4). When God laughs, his people sing![5] When I lose sight of God's sovereignty, I also lose my grip on worship. And when worship slips away, hope goes with it.

Because God is who He says He is, I can be what He calls me to be and do what He calls me to do.

In the first refrain, the nightly return of David's predators ("they come back," v. 6) is met regularly by God's sovereign chuckle ("But you," v. 8). In the second refrain there is a subtle change, for "they come back" gives way to "But I" (vv. 14, 16). Don't miss it: "But *you* . . ." becomes "But *I* . . ." Somewhere in the darkness of betrayal's pain, we are able through prayer to remember that we can do what God says we can do. Because God is who He says He is, I can be what He calls me to be and do what He calls me to do. Betrayal distorts my view of the future, but the spiritual discipline of hope illuminates the darkness of despair.

The stabbing pain of betrayal threatens to distort our perception of God, our circumstances and our future. But the spiritual disciplines of worship, confident prayer and deliberate hope restore reality to our hearts.

In his dark night of despair, David's faith rallied: "I will watch for you" . . . "I will sing praises to you" (vv. 9, 17). James Montgomery Boice notes, "In the Hebrew the words *watch* and *sing* are identical except for one letter, which is a way of saying, I suppose, that keeping one's eyes on God is only a stroke away from singing his praises and otherwise rejoicing in him." [6]

As we pray through the pains of life, no one discipline is more essential than that of keeping God accurately and squarely before the eyes of our hearts—and doing so again and again in faith. With Him there, reality begins to come into focus again, rest returns to our hearts and hope rends the dark veil of betrayal's pain.

Praying Through

Before you move on to other pursuits, sit in quiet stillness before God. Pray, following the pattern of Psalm 59:

- Begin by recounting the pain of betrayal you feel. Name the person. Express the emotion.

- Tell God the way you are tempted to see Him as inactive, blind or asleep in your situation. Having done so, turn instead to praise, recounting the names and titles and attributes of God. Use Psalm 59 as a suggestive launching point for your praise.

• Tell God how overwhelming and inescapable this mess feels. Then affirm in confident prayer that God is your fortress and that His sovereignty rules your life.

• Honestly admit to God how final this painful betrayal feels. Then deliberately lay hold of God's promises for a new day, one full of His love and of new strength.

• Finish by affirming to God that your eyes are upon Him, that you watch for Him instead of your pain or betrayer. Sing a hymn or song of confident faith.

2

Praying Through Vulnerability

A BEAD of sweat rolled down his spine as hundreds of gentile eyes stared back at him in awkward silence. David swallowed hard. He mustered a weak smile. *This is not good*, he thought, stating the obvious to himself.

It was not good, but it had seemed his only option. Racing through the darkness after leaving Michal and home behind, David had made his way north through Saul's home territory of Benjamin, toward Ramah and the old prophet Samuel. *Surely*, he'd thought to himself, *the prophet can make sense of all this.*

True enough, first the king's envoys and then the king himself had succumbed to the power of the Spirit, prophesied and were thus stymied in their pursuit. It had been a welcome reprieve and some minor consolation, but it had brought little lasting clarity to David's plight. Even the faithful commitment of Jonathan, renewed in a covenant of friendship, had failed to instill much hope.

Temporarily passing through Nob on his restless flight, David had received bread from the godly priest Ahimelech. The suddenness of his escape out the window had left him without provisions or protection. Ravenously gulping down a wad of bread, David managed to ask out of the corner of his mouth, "Don't you have a sword or spear here?" A priest's home isn't an armory, but there was the sword of Goliath that he himself had consecrated to the Lord after his acclaimed victory. Strapping it on, David tucked the bread under his arm, bid his friends goodbye and was gone. His feet carried him whatever direction appeared safest at the moment.

Thus he stood here now, in Goliath's hometown. How could this possibly be his last, best option? The giant's own sword, with which he'd beheaded the champion and of which he'd confessed "There is none like it," was strapped to his side. David let his eyes fix randomly upon faces in the crowd. Several seemed to be staring at the weapon with a knowing expression. Was the tall guy in the back a family member of the giant? Did they recognize his face from the battlefield in Socoh? Did the Hebrew folk song play through their heads, "Saul has slain his thousands, and David his tens of thousands"?

Stares. Blank, but so full of words. Another bead of sweat rolled down his back. A prepubescent boy shuffled his feet in the dust. A bent, old woman shifted the weight of her water jar. A greasy Philistine warrior rested his hand on the butt of his sword. From somewhere in the distance David heard the moan of a lonely dove. From deep within himself something seemed to reply, "Amen."[1]

• • • • •

It takes no great ability to achieve vulnerability. We manage to end up there quite regularly. You can arrive at vulnerability by either of two paths, and which one you travel in large part determines how you feel about your arrival.

A cat we once owned taught me that. Oreo was her name—
a black and white cat, as you might imagine. If I approached Oreo in a brusk fashion, reaching down and flip-
ping her on her back, I inevitably ended up with claw marks
up and down my forearm. If, however, I proceeded slowly,
gently, matching my motions with soothing, soft-toned
words, I just might manage to get Oreo to expose her belly
and almost beg me to scratch it. Same goal for me, a very
different response from her.

Ask someone to do a word-association for the word vulnerable and you are likely to hear terms like: defenseless,
exposed, helpless, powerless,
insecure, susceptible or weak.
To be vulnerable is to be open
and liable to attack. Some today refer to it as being "at
risk." For example, "at risk"

*Times of vulnerability make
communion with God a
challenge.*

children are those whose living situations, for various reasons, expose them to significant danger.

As Psalm 56 opens, we realize quickly that David was
"at risk." He had been thrust into vulnerability, not wooed
into it. Times of vulnerability make communion with God
a challenge.

When last we were with David, he was hunkered down,
trying to escape Saul's men who had surrounded his home
at night in order to kill him. After Michal lowered him
down from a window in the city wall, David began a wild
flight which brought him to Samuel at Ramah. David and
the aging prophet moved on to Naioth. Having received
word of David's whereabouts, Saul sent three different
search parties after him. Each time, however, the death

squads were overcome by the Spirit and turned into prophets. Saul himself came and he too prophesied, stripping
off his clothes and lying naked before Samuel all day and
night. David took the opportunity to flee again.

His course took him to Jonathan where the two sealed
a covenant of friendship. Soon enough, however, David
was again on the run, casting panicked glances over his
shoulder. He looked for any place that might provide some
sense of security. He found his way to Nob where his friend
Ahimelech was priest. The surprised friend's first question was, "Why are you alone, and no one with you?" (1
Sam. 21:1).

David wove a tale about top-secret kingdom business,
with information on a need-to-know basis only. The matter was so urgent that he'd been forced to leave without
weapon or supplies. The faithful priest quickly gave David
the sacred bread of the Presence and delivered over to
him the only weapon at hand—the sword David himself
had retrieved from the Philistine champion Goliath and
had used to remove his head.

David's next move was so bizarre that it can only testify
to his feeling of utter insecurity: "And David rose and fled
that day from Saul and went to Achish the king of Gath.
And the servants of Achish said to him, 'Is not this David
the king of the land? Did they not sing to one another of
him in dance, "Saul has struck down his thousands, and
David his ten thousands"?'" (1 Sam. 21:10–11).

Here is the epitome of vulnerability. Gath was Goliath's
hometown. David was the notorious killer of their "golden
boy." Strapped to David's thigh was Goliath's own sword.
And among whom did David slay most of his "ten thou-

sands," if not among the Philistines? When the safest place
you can imagine is in the midst of your greatest enemy,
you qualify for "at risk" status!

Psalm 56

*To the choirmaster: according to The Dove on Far-off Terebinths. A
Miktam of David, when the Philistines seized him in Gath.*

> *¹ Be gracious to me, O God, for man tramples on me;*
> *all day long an attacker oppresses me;*
> *² my enemies trample on me all day long,*
> *for many attack me proudly.*
> *³ When I am afraid,*
> *I put my trust in you.*
> *⁴ In God, whose word I praise,*
> *in God I trust; I shall not be afraid.*
> *What can flesh do to me?*

The title to the psalm informs us that it was to be performed according to "The Dove on Far-off Terebinths."
The exact tune is lost to us now, but you can guess from
the title that it was performed in a minor key. Like a dove
far from home, pining away in the branches of a foreign
oak, David felt like one compelled to flee to a strange land.
At times the Scriptures hold the dove before us as a symbol of suffering innocence.[2] The profile certainly fit in
David's case.

In the psalm placed immediately before this one, David
cried "Oh, that I had wings like a dove! I would fly away
and be at rest" (Ps. 55:6). All he could do then was wish for
wings to lift him from his vulnerability and place him in
some more secure dwelling place. Yet as Psalm 56 unfolds

we discover that David was able to spread his wings of faith and catch the wind of the Spirit. Though not yet physically removed from the threat that surrounded him, David was lifted up out of his troubles. In so doing David demonstrates that praying through vulnerability is possible and begins with acknowledging our fear.

Acknowledging Fear

Upon seeing his reception among the citizens of Gath and hearing them recount the victory song sung in Israel about him, David gulped hard. "And David took these words to heart and was much afraid of Achish the king of Gath" (1 Sam. 21:12). No kidding! But we need to dig deeper to understand the extent of David's extremity. This is the only time in Scripture that we are told David feared anyone but God. David had never been this low before. This was unexplored territory, a terrain he'd hoped never to see. In his prayer he cried, "When I am afraid" (v. 3), using the same Hebrew word employed in First Samuel 21:12 to describe his fear. When David hit bottom he decided anything but utter honesty about his emotions was pretense: "Be gracious to me, O God, for man tramples on me; all day long an attacker oppresses me; my enemies trample on me all day long, for many attack me proudly" (vv. 1–2).

We have trouble, even in our worst moments, with being that honest in prayer. Note the repetitions that signal David's view of those surrounding him.

My enemies are dogged: "man tramples on me," "my enemies trample on me." The word translated "trample" also has the sense of being pursued. It can describe a dog gasp-

ing, panting after its prey.[3] Ever felt the hot breath of ravenous wolves breathing down your neck?
My enemies are vicious: "an attacker oppresses me," "many
attack me proudly." Underscore "many." Saul, the armies
and citizenry of Israel, the Philistines in general, the
Gathites in particular and Achish's men most especially—
it seemed everyone wanted David's head! The word translated "proudly" has the notion of height or loftiness to it.
Was this an ironic play on words in reference to the almost
superhuman height of Goliath?[4] Remember, Goliath wasn't
the only giant in Gath (2 Sam. 21:22). Were others standing at the back of the crowd, looking down upon David?
My enemies are relentless: "all day long . . . all day long"
(vv. 1, 2; cf. v. 5). Never a moment for rest.

> [5] *All day long they injure my cause;*
>   *all their thoughts are against me for evil.*
> [6] *They stir up strife, they lurk;*
>   *they watch my steps,*
>   *as they have waited for my life.*
> [7] *For their crime will they escape?*
>   *In wrath cast down the peoples, O God!*

What made David emote in this way? *They twist my words*:
"All day long they twist my words" (v. 5).[5] The verbal form
is intensive, signaling "they utterly distort my words." This
was no mere misunderstanding but a trap intentionally
set. *They plot against me*: "all their thoughts are against me
for evil" (v. 5b). *They gang up on me*: "They stir up strife, they
lurk" (v. 6a). *They spy upon me*: "they watch my steps, as
they have waited for my life" (v. 6).

Were such feelings accurate? No doubt they were in David's situation. Are they accurate every time we feel them? Not necessarily, but they are still *ours*. And there is no praying through vulnerability until we are able to acknowledge those feelings. Feelings are strange things. They don't have to be accurate to be influential. We need to pray through to the place where we know whether we are emoting in ways appropriate to the facts, but we'll never get to that place without first acknowledging what in fact we are feeling.

> *We need to pray through to the place where we know whether we are emoting in ways appropriate to the facts, but we'll never get to that place without first acknowledging what in fact we are feeling.*

It is instructive to lay David's struggle with fear alongside Saul's concurrent slavery to fear. Saul began his reign in fear of the people he was to lead (1 Sam. 15:24). In one of his first campaigns as commander-in-chief, his fear of Goliath is noted (17:11), even as David's bravery won the day. With the groundswell of popular support for David, Saul grew afraid of him (18:12, 15). As David's success grew, so Saul's fear of him intensified (18:29). Saul's fear grew so acute that he ended up turning to a witch for help rather than expressing his fear to God (28:5)! How much better to own our fears and feelings (legitimate or not) and resolve them before God, than to deny them and be consumed by them. It was, even for a warrior like David, "*When* I am afraid," not "*if* I am afraid." The answer for the inevitability of fear is in Psalm 56:3: "I will trust in you."

Applying Faith

This reminds us that praying through vulnerability requires far more than a therapeutic acknowledgment of our emotions to God; it requires applying our faith as well. Faith reveals to us, that despite the press of our extremities, we have choices. Our first choice involves where we place our trust. "I will *put* my trust in Thee. . . In God I have *put* my trust" (vv. 3–4, NASB). Faith is something you place, not something that possesses you. Praying through vulnerability means recognizing that you possess the power to *place* your trust—as Derek Kidner puts it, "Faith is seen here as a deliberate act, in defiance of one's emotional state."[6] David, you'll notice, did not fixate upon his fears. Rather he fixed his gaze upon God.

We are not always able to choose our emotions. They are, at least initially, simply there. We can, however, choose whether or not to feed them. No matter how strong the feelings, we have the power of choice over them. We feed emotions by fixating upon them, playing scenarios over in our mind, and playing "What if . . . ?" We must find the balance of honest recognition of our emotions and the faith-filled choice to starve them. We starve illegitimate and unhealthy emotion by taking the energy and attention of worry away from them and turning it into praise and trust in God and His word (v. 4). Both honesty about and ruthlessness with our emotions is required.

We live in such an emotion-dominated world that I feel compelled to say: *this works.* You are, by God's grace, able to do this. It works in real life. In fact verse 4 is picked up by Psalm 118:6, which in turn is quoted in Hebrews 13:5–

6 in the context of anxiety about financial and material needs. This works no matter what you're facing.

This refrain of faith (vv. 3–4) is picked up again later in the prayer: "In God, whose word I praise, in the LORD, whose word I praise, in God I trust; 'I shall not be afraid. What can man do to me?'" (vv. 10–11). Notice that twice David runs from the fluctuating world of emotion (vv. 1–3, 5–7) to the fixed foundation of God's Word (vv. 4, 10). By "word" David may mean all the Scriptures recorded up to that time, or he may be more specifically referring to Samuel's word of promise about his ruling Israel one day.[7]

> *⁸You have kept count of my tossings;*
> *put my tears in your bottle.*
> *Are they not in your book?*
> *⁹Then my enemies will turn back*
> *in the day when I call.*
> *This I know, that God is for me.*
> *¹⁰In God, whose word I praise,*
> *in the LORD, whose word I praise,*
> *¹¹in God I trust; I shall not be afraid.*
> *What can man do to me?*

Notice what this word has convinced him of, and notice how David turned this faith back to God in prayer.

God, you know where I am: "You have kept count of my tossings" (v. 8). The word translated "tossings" can also be translated "wanderings."[8] It points to the aimless fugitive, stumbling in flight from his pursuers. David's frenzied flight has taken him most recently from Gibeah to Rama to Nob to Gath to . . . who knows where. It had been a roller coaster of emotion, but through it all David was convinced that God had "kept count" (a mathematical term) of his wanderings.[9] *God, you know every tear I shed*: "You have . . . put my tears in your bottle. Are they not in your book?" (v. 8). Our words "wanderings" and "tears" represent two different Hebrew words in the original, but these two words, while different, were pronounced the same.[10] No matter where your circumstances take you, God knows; no matter what pain they cause, God keeps a record of your grief. *God, you are for me*: "This I know, that God is for me" (v. 9). Though all the world be against me, God is for me. This has always been the cry of the people of faith, no matter what the extremity. "What then shall we say to these things? If God is for us, who can be against us?" (Rom. 8:31).

Applying your faith in prayer means choosing your trust. The object of our trust must be God Himself. The foundation and fuel of such faith must be the words of God. Applying your faith in prayer, however, requires another choice. We must choose our emotions as well as our trust.

We are not always able to select our initial feelings when confronted by fearful circumstances. We can, however, choose the emotions we continue the journey with.

It's true that we are not always able to select our initial feelings. They simply come upon us. We are, however, able to choose the emotions we continue the journey with. An amazing realization comes to us when we re-read verses 3 and 4, but this time eat them like an Oreo (not the cat this time!). Take them apart, remove the middle and then put the two chocolate cookies back together. Here is what we

end up with: "When I am afraid . . . I shall not be afraid"!
Is that possible? The therapy-model of Christianity tells
you it is not. The trust-model of Christianity bellows a
resounding "Yes!"

Emotions can be harnessed, controlled and brought into
submission. To do so we must put them on a tether. Picture it like a water skier. When the boat turns the skier
inevitably follows the same path, though not instantly.
There is a time delay. The process is not instantaneous,
but it is inevitable. You are in the boat, and your choices
of faith have the power to turn the wheel. Your emotions,
while very real, are along for the ride. Too many people
think the skier (emotion) pulls the boat, when in fact it is
the boat (faith-filled choices based upon God's Word) that
ultimately steers the skier. God's grace, by the Spirit and
through his Word, enables you to choose, not necessarily
your initial emotions, but the ones you bring along for the
journey.

Articulating Faith

Only after acknowledging feelings and applying faith,
are we ready to look accurately at the object of our fear:
"What can flesh do to me? . . . What can man do to me?"
(vv. 4, 11). Addressed in this order we are ready to say,
"This I know, that God is for me" (v. 9). This declaration
of faith is picked up in the New Testament and made part
of one of the greatest statements of faith ever made:

> What then shall we say to these things? If God is for us,
> who can be against us? . . . Who shall separate us from the
> love of Christ? Shall tribulation, or distress, or persecu-

tion, or famine, or nakedness, or danger, or sword? . . . No, in all these things we are more than conquerors through him who loved us. For I am sure that neither death nor life, nor angels nor rulers, nor things present nor things to come, nor powers, nor height nor depth, nor anything else in all creation, will be able to separate us from the love of God in Christ Jesus our Lord. (Romans 8:31, 35, 37–39)

Indeed, an articulation of faith is how David closed his prayer:

> *12 I must perform my vows to you, O God;*
> *I will render thank offerings to you.*
> *13 For you have delivered my soul from death,*
> *yes, my feet from falling,*
> *that I may walk before God*
> *in the light of life.*

The tense of the verb tells it all: "you *have delivered* my soul." It's a done deal. Not yet in experience, but in the eyes (and on the tongue) of faith. We must articulate in prayer the faith we have chosen. The word from God that we have believed and banked on must become the prayer we hold before God in faith. We often pray like defeated people. We do indeed need to be authentic about our fears, but we must also emerge out of that fear and utter prayers of faith. We seem to waver at one of two extremes in our praying. We pray faithless prayers, wallowing in and whining about our troubles. Or we pray thoughtless prayers, mindlessly parroting pious sounding phrases without thinking deeply about what they mean. We must be genuine with God about our feelings, but we must also pick up specific promises of God and tenaciously implore that they be made actual in our case.

David's goal was not simply to feel better (though that is a powerful motivation in such dire circumstances), but that "I may walk before God in the light of life" (v. 13). Intimate knowledge of God is the goal, an intimate knowledge of God that is actively fleshed out in obedience ("walk").

Interestingly David's last phrase found its way to the lips of Jesus. "I am the light of the world. Whoever follows me will not walk in darkness, but will have *the light of life*" (John 8:12). This means, of course, that the ultimate answer to David's prayer is realized in us. It is answered in our most vulnerable state, the darkness of our sin, when Jesus Christ delivers us and then walks with us in every dark moment that follows in the journey of faith ahead. Jesus Himself is "the light of life." He promises us Himself as the ultimate answer to our prayer.

When the circumstances of life force us into a position of vulnerability, our normal reaction is to fight back. Such self-defense can cause us to shut down even toward God, perhaps wondering why He has allowed such pain to enter our lives. But if we listen with different ears, we may just find that the circumstances He has allowed announce a different message, an invitation to intimacy rather than a hint of His withdrawing from us. Perhaps, by allowing the forced vulnerability of circumstances, He is wooing us to a willing vulnerability with Himself. If our goal is God, no circumstance can derail us from our objective. With Him we may pray, "This I know, that God is for me" and thus "When I am afraid . . . I will not be afraid" (vv. 9, 3–4).

Praying Through

Before you move on to other pursuits, take several minutes with God to pray through your feelings of vulnerability. Use the pattern of Psalm 56 as your guide:

- Spend some time authentically describing your fears to God. Name the object of your fear. Be descriptive about the emotions. Don't hesitate to be genuine. Let them be heard in your voice, seen in your gestures and demonstrated in your tears if need be.

- Transition now, and declare to God by faith (not necessarily with the backing of your feelings yet) that you choose to trust Him. Name the people or circumstances that you are entrusting to Him. Recount to God that you know He is aware of your circumstances and tears, and that He is for you. Choose the object of your trust.

- Finally, declare to God that "When I am afraid of _____, I will not allow my fear to immobilize me!" Rise up in faith and tell God that your ultimate objective is not to feel better but to walk more closely with Him. Thank Him that nothing can derail you from that objective, not even your current circumstances.

3

Praying Through Humiliation

DAVID STOOD frozen under the heat of the Philistine sun. Not even the fire of a thousand pagan eyes burning a hole through him could melt his statuesque pose. Even his mind seemed immobilized by the fear, his thoughts put on hold as if someone pushed a "pause" button on his brain. How long had he stood immobile?

Suddenly, as awaking from a stupor, a thought broke the trance—a thought so ordinary, so mundane that the recognition of it at a moment like this seemed ludicrous. But it came with a swell of hope. It was simply the sudden conscious recognition of another bead of sweat cascading down his spine.

The sensation suggested a possible escape. *That's it! It's the only way,* the would-be king's heart shouted to itself.

Slowly David began to turn down the right corner of his mouth and held it there until a stream of drool began to suspend itself from his lower lip. It caught in his beard and hung there momentarily, until the weight of the flow sent it to the ground.

The right eyebrow of a Philistine commander arched in an expression of puzzled query.

David added a wide-eyed, wild look to his countenance.

A little boy in the crowd clutched at his mother's skirt and shifted behind her, leaving only two frightened eyes peering round her hip. She too noticed the oddity and placed her hand softly, but firmly around his shoulder— as if to reassure him of her protection.

A quick jerk of his head and a quirky gesture with his hand was followed by a palsied hunch and step. David was in full theatric form now. His performance was not wasted on the crowd. Everyone took an uneasy step back. David interspersed a few incoherent groans as he continued his one-act play, his one-man show.

The eyes of several soldiers shifted toward King Achish. The monarch squinted, half in disgust and half in a studied suspicion.

David was getting his desired response, but he would have to up the ante to achieve his goal. Spying a sharply pointed stone about a foot in front of the surrounding crowd, David lunged at it with a violent leap capable of scaring the hair off a jackal's back.

Several women gave out shrill shrieks as the entire populace of Gath drew back from the madman. David paused, turning from the brusk movement that had seized the stone, now almost adoring it, holding it fondly in both hands as if it were a new-found pet. Without taking his gaze off the treasured stone, David moved toward the city gate about twenty yards distant. The crowd parted as if an infectious disease was blowing down the street. Eyes widened as Israel's greatest warrior continued his quirky and odd shuffle, saliva cascading in a steady stream out his mouth, down his beard and into the dust.

Reaching his destination, David caressed the pillar to which one of the gates was attached. Women held their hands over their mouths. Children turned the look of a thousand questions in the direction of their fathers. Slowly, almost with artistic flair, David began to scribble with the point of the stone. Eyes drew together. Heads leaned forward. Every mind began trying to decipher the lines and shapes that began to form on the pillar of the city's gates. The collective silence was broken by a deep bellowing voice.

"Enough! Enough!" cried Achish. "Why do you bring me such a mental case? Do I lack morns? Obviously not!"

Horses jerked and pulled back at their reigns. Soldiers snapped to attention.

"Get him out of my presence!" the king ordered.

With that a solider swung the city gates open and stepped back. David dropped his treasured stone, abandoned his artwork and again began his grotesque shuffle. As he exited beyond the city walls, the Gathites seemed to exhale a deep, communal sigh of relief. Without anyone saying so, everyone knew this would provide conversation around nighttime fires and dinner tables for weeks.

Knowing that eyes were still fixed upon him, David continued his mumbling conversation with himself as he made his way across the open plain in front of the city. His arms flailed as he took the halting steps of a village idiot. David fixed his eyes on a grove of trees a half-mile or so before him. He had to keep the performance up just a little longer. Just as it appeared he might actually escape, a bitter combination of satisfaction and utter humiliation rose within him. Had this all really just happened? As the trees drew nearer, relief faded and a heavy wave of shame swept over David.

The drool ceased flowing from his mouth, but tears began to form in the corners of his eyes.[1]

• • • • •

What's the stupidest thing you've ever done? It's the question raised when the party turns dull. We enjoy the stupidity of others vicariously. There's not much celebration, however, when the question circles around to us. Occasionally the passing of time allows us to chuckle even over our own blunders, but often the pain lasts a lifetime. I recall standing in an emergency room beside a young man who had just permanently maimed his body through a foolish, youthful accident. Through the pain and the drugs given to dull it, the only words that rose from his lips were, "I am so stupid. I am so stupid. I am so . . ."

Life's stupidest moments are not often things we celebrate. That's why the reverent revelry of Psalm 34 seems so out of step with its title. Amazingly, David's greatest humiliation had become one of his most profound moments of fellowship with God.

Historically speaking Psalm 34 follows on the heels of Psalm 56. We left David standing awkwardly in the presence of the citizenry of Goliath's hometown, wearing the giant's sword. He found himself staring at family members of many he'd slain in battle. What had seemed his last best option moments before, now had gone terribly wrong. David knew the next few moments would determine the longevity of his life.

In the tense silence of the moment, David formulated a plan. Seeing the less-than-favorable reception by King Achish, David "changed his behavior before them and pretended to be insane in their hands and made marks on the doors of the gate and let his spittle run down his beard"

(1 Sam. 21:13). Don't miss how profoundly desperate this move was. This was the "boy wonder" of Israel who had stood toe-to-toe with Philisita's greatest warrior when no one else dared to take him on. David had not counted his life dear when the name of the Lord had been ridiculed. Yet here he was now playing the part of the village idiot to save his own skin! David had fled not simply to Gentile territory, but to the far reaches of desperation.

You'll note that no subtlety of David's performance was lost on the king, who bellowed, "Behold, you see the man is mad. . . . Do I lack madmen, that you have brought this fellow to behave as a madman in my presence?" (21:14). David's theatrics were skillful and successful, but they were also humiliating and foolish.

What do you do after the stupidest thing you've ever done? Simple. You hide. "David escaped from there to the cave of Adullam" (1 Sam. 22:1). Linger over that for a moment: **HIDE**. Those who can pinpoint their stupidest moment know just what it represents:

> **H**umiliation
> **I**ndignity
> **D**isgrace
> **E**mbarrassment

Certainly David felt all of that and more. Yet somehow, in the deep recesses of that cave, God transformed the stupidest thing David ever did into a summons to worship and a lesson in wisdom.

A Summons to Worship

The goodness of God that David tasted, not only in his escape from Gath, but in the hours of fellowship with God that followed in the cave of Adullam, became a deep call to worship.

─────⟾─────

When you've done something stupid, run to God rather than from Him. It will result in a celebration of God's goodness instead of a rehearsal of your stupidity.

While David hid himself physically, he realized that trying to hide spiritually would only put him in even greater danger. The reflex to do so was surely there, but he knew the results would have been devastating. So David ran to God, rather than from Him. The result was a celebration of God's goodness instead of a rehearsal of his stupidity.

Psalm 34

Of David, when he changed his behavior before Abimelech,[2] so that he drove him out, and he went away.

> *¹ I will bless the LORD at all times;*
> *his praise shall continually be in my mouth.*
> *² My soul makes its boast in the LORD;*
> *let the humble hear and be glad.*
> *³ Oh, magnify the LORD with me,*
> *and let us exalt his name together!*
>
> *⁴ I sought the LORD, and he answered me*
> *and delivered me from all my fears.*
> *⁵ Those who look to him are radiant,*
> *and their faces shall never be ashamed.*

David knew that worship, especially at such low moments, requires commitment. Listen to the resolve in his voice: "*I will* bless the LORD *at all times*; his praise *shall continually be* in my mouth. My soul makes its boast in the LORD; let the humble hear and be glad. Oh, *magnify the LORD with me*, and let us exalt his name together!" (vv. 1–3). Worship requires more than feelings of well-being; it runs on commitment to the glory of God. In fact it is this preoccupation with and commitment to God's glory, rather than your image, that is the key to overcoming your shame ("Those who look to him are radiant, and their faces shall never be ashamed," v. 5).

Helen Keller once said, "Unless we form the habit of going to the Bible in bright moments as well as in trouble, we cannot fully respond to its consolations because we lack equilibrium between light and darkness." David, long before the folly of his feigned madness in Gath, had formed the holy habit of worship.

> **6** *This poor man cried, and the LORD heard him*
> *and saved him out of all his troubles.*
> **7** *The angel of the LORD encamps*
> *around those who fear him, and delivers them.*
>
> **8** *Oh, taste and see that the LORD is good!*
> *Blessed is the man who takes refuge in him!*

This was far more than "I guess I'd better go to church." Worship will rarely rise above drudgery for those motivated only by discipline and commitment. David had tasted the goodness of God (v. 8) and the sweet aftertaste forever flavored his expressions of praise. If prayer is a pain, if worship has become nothing but work, if devotion is a drudgery, then you have reason to wonder if you've really ever been reduced to that place of utter humility. For only there can we drink deeply enough of God's grace to never forget its taste. It is at those depths that the facade drops away, and we are exposed to God. When we discover that even there God is good and that He still loves, receives and forgives, we are finally ready to worship. Now worship is motivated not simply by commitment but by grace. It takes such deep grace to move us beyond the necessary discipline of worship to the glad delight of worship.

Commitment leads us to the Lord's presence in worship, but it is contemplation that brings us into actual fellowship with Him. Notice the past tenses as David reviews what God has done for him: "*I sought* the LORD, and *he answered* me and *delivered* me from all my fears. . . . This poor man *cried*, and the LORD *heard* him and *saved* him out of all his troubles" (vv. 4–6). The fingers of contemplation have taken over for sheer commitment in plucking the strings of worship.[3] Note the conclusion drawn from his reflection on God's grace: "The angel of the LORD encamps around those who fear him, and delivers them" (v. 7).

Who is this "angel of the LORD"? He is the One whose voice stopped Abraham as he raised the knife to sacrifice his son (Gen. 22:11), who protected Jacob (Gen. 31:11), met Moses in the burning bush (Ex. 3:2) and led the Israelites through the wilderness in a pillar of cloud and fire (Exod. 14:19, 23:20). This is the One who handed Moses the commandments on Sinai (Acts 6:38), reassured Joshua before the battle of Jericho (Josh. 5:13–15), and would later fellowship with Daniel's three friends in the fiery furnace (Dan. 3:24–25). He is the One who would later be designated "the son of David" (Matt. 1:1), claim the throne of David (Rev. 22:16) and as the Good Shepherd would lay down His life for the sheep (John 10:11). He is the One who, having been raised from the dead, would promise, "I am with you always, to the end of the age" (Matt. 28:20). This angel of the Lord was, according to the chorus raised by a vast throng of interpreters, the pre-incarnate Christ Himself.[4]

How is that possible? Simply because there are depths of grace and an intimacy of fellowship only possible to those who worship God at the depths of their stupidest moments.

In the 1830s a British naturalist named Edward Forbes, after studying the depths of the Atlantic and Mediterranean, declared that no life existed in the seas below 2,000 feet. The pressure, it was presumed, was simply too much. Pressure on the ocean's floor is so extreme that it would equal 300 jumbo jets set upon a man's chest. No one can survive at such depths and under such pressures. A mere thirty years later, a crew repairing transatlantic telegraph cables hauled up portions of the line from over two miles down. To everyone's surprise they found it covered with living creatures.[5]

So, too, we quickly conclude that we will never survive the depths of humiliation. We declare the pressures of stupidity unlivable. But those who turn to God in worship at such moments find not only that life is livable, but that there is a quality of spiritual life that can be had in no other place.

Our initial worship by commitment gives way to glad, contemplative worship, which in turn gives way to a deeply contented worship:

> **⁸** *Oh, taste and see that the LORD is good!*
>   *Blessed is the man who takes refuge in him!*
> **⁹** *Oh, fear the LORD, you his saints,*
>   *for those who fear him have no lack!*

The Authorized Version renders that last expression "There is no want."

Honesty forces us to ask, *Is such contentment even possible in an age that feeds our appetite for "more" by incessant sound bytes, billboards, radio spots, TV commercials and web page pop-ups?* Factor in our own greed, gluttony and avarice, along with all the deficits exposed in our stupidest moments, and we are compelled to ask, *Is it possible to actually live at the level of "no want"?*

It is, but it begins with the realization that "no want" is not the same as "want nothing." Worshipers may not possess all they want, but they never lack all they truly need. Indeed they find their desires transformed and conformed to the will of God, so that then they actually want what He provides (Ps. 37:4). This land of "no want" is arrived at by a curiously circuitous route:

> **¹⁰** *The young lions suffer want and hunger;*
>   *but those who seek the LORD lack no good thing.*

Hungry lions hunt when they lack (v. 10). But, says David, "those who seek the Lord [rather than the feeding

of their appetites] lack no good thing" (v. 10). Contentment comes not through superior effort, and certainly not
because of superior intelli-
gence (David's actions prove
that!). God is the provider,
not our energies or our inge-
nuities. God calls us to focus
both our labor and logic
upon Him, but ultimately it
is the "fear of the LORD" (vv.
7, 9, 11) that releases the pro-
vision of God into our lives. The fear of man led David to
his lowest moment (v. 4), but it was the fear of the Lord
that lifted him out of it. [6]

> *The fear of the Lord releases the*
> *provision of God into our lives.*
> *The fear of man led David to*
> *his lowest moment, but it was*
> *the fear of the Lord that*
> *lifted him out of it.*

> [11] *Come, O children, listen to me;*
>   *I will teach you the fear of the LORD.*
> [12] *What man is there who desires life*
>   *and loves many days, that he may see good?*
> [13] *Keep your tongue from evil*
>   *and your lips from speaking deceit.*
> [14] *Turn away from evil and do good;*
>   *seek peace and pursue it.*

A Summons to Wisdom

All of this has been about worship, but the prayer shifts
now to the theme of wisdom. David moved from song to
sermon. So must we. God's goodness is not simply a call to
worship but also a summons to walk in wisdom. Such
worship and wisdom are first aroused by taste of God's
grace at our lowest moments (v. 8) and then taught by those

willing to learn from their lowest moments (v. 11). This means wisdom requires our participation. We must learn from our mistakes. The fact that we must *learn* the fear of the Lord reminds us that none of us is naturally wise. My most embarrassing moments are not inexplicable events blemishing an otherwise stellar record. The stupidest things I've ever done only reveal my true colors. None of us will arrive at wisdom on our own. We must be led there . . . by God. As we are willing to process our failures with God through reflective and attentive prayer, He redeems them for good by helping us learn from them. He teaches us what to say ("Keep your tongue from evil and your lips from speaking deceit," v. 13), what to do ("Turn away from evil and do good," v. 14) and what to pursue ("seek peace and pursue it," v. 14).

> [15] *The eyes of the LORD are toward the righteous*
>   *and his ears toward their cry.*
> [16] *The face of the LORD is against those who do evil,*
>   *to cut off the memory of them from the earth.*
> [17] *When the righteous cry for help, the LORD hears*
>   *and delivers them out of all their troubles.*
> [18] *The LORD is near to the brokenhearted*
>   *and saves the crushed in spirit.*
>
> [19] *Many are the afflictions of the righteous,*
>   *but the LORD delivers him out of them all.*
> [20] *He keeps all his bones;*
>   *not one of them is broken.*
> [21] *Affliction will slay the wicked,*
>   *and those who hate the righteous will be condemned.*
> [22] *The LORD redeems the life of his servants;*
>   *none of those who take refuge in him will be condemned.*

The great value of our stupidest moments is that they make us teachable, if we are willing. Such teachability draws God's attention. Honesty, authenticity and humility position us to learn wisdom. Not many let their low points lead them there, but when they do, God notices. If you will go there, His eyes will be upon you (v. 15), His ears will be tuned to your voice (vv. 15, 17), His face will turn toward you (v. 16) and His presence will surround you (v. 18).

The humiliated but still prideful person doubts such intimacy with God is possible; the humbled and teachable one simply enters in. The life God offers here and now is not one void of trouble, for "Many are the afflictions of the righteous" (v. 19). But it is one in which He actively, constantly and intimately takes a part. He offers to unleash His power on our behalf as we strive for His glory. The choice is ours. Your existence can prove that "Affliction will slay the wicked, and those who hate the righteous will be condemned" (v. 21) or that "The LORD redeems the life of his servants; none of those who take refuge in him will be condemned" (v. 22). Take your pick. Your willingness to linger with God and pray through your humiliation is how you functionally make your choice.

God doesn't promise to erase your stupidest moment from the annals of history, but He will redeem it. In fact He already has. David prayed, "He keeps all his bones; not one of them is broken" (v. 20). That, in the Spirit-inspired view of the Apostle John, pointed ultimately to Jesus as He offered Himself in atonement for our sins on the cross (John 19:36). I look back and obsess over past failures wondering, "Why did I?" Jesus looked forward to my worst moments and declared, "Put them to my account." All the stupid, sinful things I have done, He anticipated and bore the consequences of on the cross. Jesus went to His lowest point (even to death) so that my lowest moment doesn't have to be the end of my story.

My life to this point has proven one thing: Given enough time, I'm going to do something stupid. Eventually, all of us let our true colors show. God's suggestion sounds something like this: "Let's be honest right up front. You need Me. I love you. I've made a way for both My love and your need to be fulfilled. Come to Me. Pray through. Taste and see. Let Me transform your weakness and sin into worship and wisdom."

Praying Through

Linger with God before you close the book. Pray through your humiliation, using Psalm 34 as a guide.

- Authentically express your feelings of embarrassment and humiliation to God. Do not hold back. Make the intensity of your prayer match what is on the inside. It's OK—God can take it. Exhaust yourself in honest expression to God. Don't move on until you have.

- Choose now, out of the exhaustion and emptiness of honest prayer, to worship God. You can. You must. Recount the many graces He has given you, even now, even in your worst moments. Pray through until you treasure His goodness as much as you despise your failure. Pray through to a place of rest.

- Out of a heart now awed by God's goodness, ask Him to show you what there is to learn through this failure. Lodge your request with Him and wait, even for a stretch of time, if need be. Watch for His lesson, linger over His Word. Tell Him you believe He is drawing near to you (vv. 15–18). Thank Him for redeeming your humiliation (vv. 19–22).

4

Praying Through Loneliness

SCRAMBLING UP the loose rock, David gathered his final reserves of strength and lunged forward toward the open mouth of Addulam's cave.[1] His exhausted body slapped flat on the inside lip of the cave. Using his momentum he forced himself into a roll, his limbs flopping helplessly as he pitched forward. As he disappeared into the darkness, he found the cool air a welcome relief. His body fumbled to a halt. The damp and musty air made his lungs burn as his chest heaved in frantic gasps for oxygen.

David lay immobilized, his limbs sprawled outward from his body. His eyes began to adjust to the darkness and he stared at the rock ceiling, his mind rehearsing his frantic ten-mile flight through the wilderness. When David had reached the grove of trees outside of Gath, he'd broken into a dead run, headed nowhere in particular but anywhere that left Philistine territory behind him. He once thought Goliath's hometown would be a refuge compared to the murderous pursuits of Saul's men in his homeland. Now he did not know if the greater danger lay behind or before.

Minutes melded into an hour as David lost track of

time, disabled in the darkness. Had he drifted into sleep or was this nightmare real? His muscles tightened into near paralysis as he lay motionless in the clammy chill. The stillness of his body concealed the wild, erratic ventures of his mind and heart. David replayed the last several months again and again. *Why? What have I done?*

Then, like a tidal wave arising from the core of his being and gathering momentum as it rushed up from his heart, the pent up emotion of months of unjust treatment reached his vocal chords. The long silence gave way to a ringing, inarticulate scream that vibrated off the stark cave walls. The reverberating echos mocked this anointed-of-the-Lord.

Several bats stirred in the back recesses of the cave and fluttered their way past the anguished figure now writhing on the cave floor.

"WHYYYYYYY?!?"

A second eruption found its way to the surface. His throat clenched from the sudden blasts and his cramped muscles burned as he lurched from his immobility. Bitter tears burned their way out of the corner of David's eyes and rolled down his cheeks, making miniature mud slides in the collected dust.

Finally he could release the toxin that slowly had been poisoning his spirit. Finally he was alone. Finally he could give full throat to his complaint. Finally he could be honest with himself. Finally, finally he was alone. Finally. Alone. All alone. Finally.

Yes, it certainly did feel final.

• • • • •

At the close of his troubled life Thomas Wolfe con-
cluded, "The whole conviction of my life now rests upon
the belief that loneliness, far from being a rare and curious phenomenon, peculiar to a few other solitary people,
is the central and inevitable feature of human existence."
Pollster George Gallup came to the same conclusion, al-
beit through more scientific means, "I think we are a very
lonely populace; we are cut apart from each other."

Yet for proof of the centrality and inevitability of loneliness we need go no further than the annals of popular
music. Has there been a theme more common to popular
music than loneliness? Scan just the last three decades.
Roy Orbison sang "Only the Lonely." Elvis Presely asked
"Are You Lonely Tonight?" Journey sang, "Ask the Lonely."
The Backstreet Boys demanded, "Show Me the Meaning
of Being Lonely." And Christina Aguilera admitted, "No-
body Wants to Be Lonely."

Roy Orbison perhaps put these common feelings most
classically, "Only the lonely know the way I feel tonight,
Only the lonely know this feeling ain't right." Yes, Roy,
loneliness "ain't right," but it is a fact. Ravi Zacharias has
circled the globe countless times in the cause of Christ,
and his observation is that ". . . this cry of loneliness is felt
by all, though better expressed by some."

David knew the ache of loneliness, and he expressed it
well in Psalm 142. After his desperate one-act play in Gath
and a frantic flight to the refuge of Adullam's cave, David
had never felt more alone. Behind him was bitter ethnic
resentment and personal humiliation; before him lay royal
paranoia and public disinformation. He was both surrounded and utterly alone.

Remember the words repeatedly used to describe the condition of Sadaam Hussein when American troops finally captured him? Having buried himself in a small hole to escape detection, his captors unearthed him and proclaimed to the world, "We found him hiding like a rat in a hole!"

The loneliness we feel is not pointless. God has a bigger purpose for allowing us to pass through the proviong grounds of solitude.

David, while no Sadaam Hussein, was anointed for the throne of Israel, but hiding in a hole, despised and demoralized.

A.W. Tozer said, "Most of the world's great souls have been lonely." If he was correct, then it teaches us to trust God that the loneliness we feel is not pointless; God has a bigger purpose for allowing us to pass through the proving grounds of solitude.

Psalm 142

A Maskil of David, when he was in the cave. A prayer.

> ¹ *With my voice I cry out to the LORD;*
>   *with my voice I plead for mercy to the LORD.*
> ² *I pour out my complaint before him;*
>   *I tell my trouble before him.*

Voice Your Cry

Praying through loneliness demands that you voice the cry of your heart. Note the repetitions with which David began his lament: "I cry out . . . I plead . . . I pour out my complaint . . . I tell my trouble" (vv. 1, 2). Of these four Hebrew verbs, the first is a cry for help from your distress, the second an appeal for mercy, the third a rehearsal of your complaint and the last an announcement of your pain. There is no praying through without articulating the biting pain of your sense of abandonment.

I recall well the first time my father took me hunting. We were after rabbit. I was armed with my BB gun, he with a .22 rifle. Not long out we spotted a bunny bounding across the snow in an open field. My father drew a bead and squeezed the trigger. To my utter surprise the rabbit dropped. I streaked ahead to see the results of the remarkable shot of my father. As I approached I heard something that still rings in my ears. The rabbit was not dead, but mortally wounded. Writhing in the throws of death it was emitting what can only be described as a scream. It was piercing. It sounded eerily human. With a single BB I silenced the scream but have heard it many times since in my head. It's what comes to my mind when I hear David in these opening volleys of Psalm 142.

Such a cry is never tidy, sanitary or formal. It is messy, almost uncontrolled. It is, most of all, real. And it is audible. "*With my voice* I cry out . . . *with my voice* I plead" (v. 1).

The emphasis here is on vocalized, articulated prayer. This is not introspection. This is not getting in touch with your feelings. Nor is this self-talk. The walls of the cave reverberated with David's screams. What had remained pent up for safety's sake in Gath now came thundering out in the isolation of the cave.

Actress Inger Stevens once confessed, "Sometimes I get so lonely I could scream." She was on the right track, but sadly she later took her own life. Loneliness consumes, and unless we purge it through honest prayer before God, it will finish us.

We must put audible expression to our emotions and thoughts when lonely. It must be expressed, and it must be expressed authentically. Jacques Ellul warns us of prayer that "remains unarticulated, very ardent perhaps, but without content." Like turning the switch on a lamp that has no bulb, little happens when our prayers remain wholly internal and silent. H.C. Leupold says, "There seems to be some advantage in putting trouble into words: it seems less threatening; we have its measure after we have stated it. All God's saints have found this to be the case with regard to their prayers."

People regularly recount to me the pain of their lives. As I listen I attempt to hear not simply their words but their hearts. I look for the emotion in their tone, the edge on their words, the look in their eyes, the language of their posture and gestures. Not uncommonly after someone pours out the bile of bitter emotion, I suggest that we pray. The transformation that takes place the moment we bow our heads is nothing short of astonishing. Nothing will have changed within them, but suddenly their words are measured, their emotions muted, their speech pious and sanctified. They modulate their tones and rein in their words.

On occasion I've stopped a person in mid-prayer, saying, "Listen, you're just not honest with God. A minute ago you were animated, honest and authentic. You were angry, grieved, hurt and livid. You were waving your arms, red in the face and spraying spittle around the room. You spared no expression in making certain I understood just how bad you've been hurt. Why aren't you being honest with God?"

It is "to the LORD" (twice in v. 1) and "before him" (twice in v. 2) that we must raise our cry. These cries of distress, appeals for mercy, rehearsals of complaint and reports of hardship are to be made articulate before God. Don't back off. Don't water it down. God is big enough to handle what's in your heart. You pray such prayers not to inform God, but to free your own heart. Mark this down: If you do not authentically

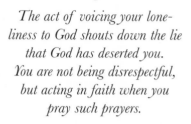

The act of voicing your loneliness to God shouts down the lie that God has deserted you. You are not being disrespectful, but acting in faith when you pray such prayers.

articulate the cry of your lonely heart, you only confirm the lie that you are alone in this. The act of voicing your cry to God is, as much as anything, a shouting down of the lie that even God has deserted you. You are not being disrespectful, but acting in faith when you pray such prayers.

> [3] *When my spirit faints within me,*
> *you know my way!*
> *In the path where I walk*
> *they have hidden a trap for me.*
> [4] *Look to the right and see:*
> *there is none who takes notice of me;*
> *no refuge remains to me;*
> *no one cares for my soul.*

Acknowledge Your Pain

David made three great confessions regarding the pain of loneliness. He admitted, *I am overwhelmed.* "When my spirit faints within me, you know my way!" (v. 3). The verb "faints" describes that which has become feeble, faint or grown weak. It describes someone overwhelmed by their circumstances. Jonah used the same word when he prayed from the belly of the fish: "When my life *was fainting away,* I remembered the LORD, and my prayer came to you . . ." (Jon. 2:7).

This word always conjures up images of a scene in the movie *The Perfect Storm.* Fishing boat captain Billy Tyne has taken his men too far out—all the way to the Flemish Cap—too late in the season. A hurricane moving northward from Bermuda and a massive storm descending from the north collide to create the storm of the century. Tyne's vessel, the Andrea Gail, becomes helplessly caught in the perfect storm. After bravely battling gargantuan waves, the ship is finally overcome by a massive sea swell. With the ship now upside down and descending to the depths, only crew member Bobby Shatford is able to escape the sinking vessel. In a moving scene the camera pans back from the helpless, solitary figure bobbing in the tumultuous waters of the angry North Atlantic without even a life vest. Clearly he is at the mercy of the storm. His fate is sealed, and only moments stand between him and the inevitable. Soon enough he will be overwhelmed by the power of the storm and slip below the waterline, erasing all evidence of his existence. The powerful emotions of utter and complete aloneness sweep over the audience.

Know that emotion? Loneliness can create that. It leaves you feeling cut off from everyone, everything . . . even God. At such moments you feel the only strength, wisdom and resources are those which lie within you. There is no one to watch your back, hold your hand or lift you up. You are alone.

That has to be expressed—in all the honesty of its powerful emotion—to God.

David also confessed, *I am used.* "In the path where I walk they have hidden a trap for me" (v. 3b). The only ones showing any interest in you are those who want to use you. The telemarketers, the hucksters, the sham-artists, the users. They know your number, they call you by name. But there is always an agenda, a catch, strings attached. How well Jesus knew that feeling. Plenty of folks wanted to ride the groundswell of popular support for Christ, so they could market their pre-existing agendas. As I write I'm picturing faces, could recite their names and recount to you what they wanted my friendship for. I'll not list them here, but I have had to express it all to Christ—including the anger, bitterness and vengeance that goes with the memories.

In fact just this morning my wife's purse was stolen. Beyond the sense of violation was the reminder that, to at least someone, we are worth nothing but the grocery money that is now gone. To others we have been reduced to a series of numbers—credit card numbers, driver's license numbers, checking account numbers and now a police report number. There is no name. No relationship. No intimacy. Just the data of our lives. We are processed, not helped. We have a claim to file, not a cry to be heard.

David also cried, *I am abandoned.* "Look to the right and see; there is none who takes notice of me; no refuge remains to me; no one cares for my soul" (v. 4). In David's day "to the right" is where a friend or legal counsel or bodyguards would have stood. The verb "takes notice of" speaks of paying attention to someone. No one even seemed to notice that David existed. No one took note of his needs.

I am reminded of the final letter of the Apostle Paul. He was in a Roman dungeon awaiting a certain execution. Tradition tells us he was beheaded for his faith in Christ. As he penned his last communication it went to his beloved son-in-the-faith Timothy. There he confessed, "You are aware that *all* who are in Asia turned away from me" (2 Tim. 1:12). Later he added, "At my first defense *no one* came to stand by me, but *all* deserted me" (4:16). Paul's own words make clear that the words "all" and "no one" should not be taken absolutely, for he admits that Onesiphorus and his family had not deserted him (1:16). It was not literally *all*, but it felt like *all*! The key is to see that even Paul needed to express such emotions. He did so to a safe friend, but certainly had first done so to God.

Prayers expressing the pain of loneliness are often 911-prayers. They are made under duress, when we are less than our best. Our guard is down, our words are not polished and the outcome is not publishable—but it is real, and that is what matters most.

This morning as I placed the 911 call to the police regarding my wife's purse, I was reminded of the nature of this kind of prayer. I was first connected to an adjoining city's dispatcher, when she found out where I was she said,

"Stay on the line. Don't hang up. I'll connect you with the police department in your city." As I waited I began speaking to my wife and the dispatcher broke in again, instructing me, "Don't hang up. Stay on the line. Help is on the way."

That's the point of these kinds of prayers—the key is to keep the line open. The point is not how carefully crafted the words are, nor how polished and polite the verbiage. The key is to call out to God, get connected, stay connected and keep the line of communication open. When we do so, God assures us that help is on the way.

Emergency prayers need not be carefully crafted words or polished and polite verbiage. The key is to call out to God and stay connected. When we do so, God assures us that help is on the way.

Embrace Your Hope

As we pray through, expressing the pain of loneliness, we break through to a place of hope. Embracing this hope is a key component to praying completely through to the other side of loneliness. Two great promises brought hope to David. The first is, *God alone knows me*. God alone knows your feelings: "When my spirit faints within me, you know my way!" (v. 3). God alone knows your path: "In the path where I walk they have hidden a trap for me" (v. 3).

The One whose friends slept while He prayed alone to the point of sweating blood, who was betrayed to death by a friend's kiss and who stood abandoned at a rigged trial—He is the One who knows. He may be the only one who knows, but as you break through the pain of loneliness, He is enough. He is hope.

> *⁵ I cry to you, O LORD;*
> *   I say, "You are my refuge,*
> *   my portion in the land of the living."*
> *⁶ Attend to my cry,*
> *   for I am brought very low!*
> *Deliver me from my persecutors,*
> *   for they are too strong for me!*
> *⁷ Bring me out of prison,*
> *   that I may give thanks to your name!*
> *The righteous will surround me,*
> *   for you will deal bountifully with me.*

Second, David found hope in the fact that *God alone is near me.* As you meet God in your loneliness, He becomes your refuge. "I say, 'You are my refuge'" (v. 5). The word is used to describe shelter found during a rainstorm. Even during the perfect storm of your loneliness, God is a safe place to which you can run. God also becomes your rescue. "Attend to my cry, for I am brought very low! Deliver me from my persecutors, for they are too strong for me!" (v. 6). Ultimately our hope is found not in being lifted from our lonely circumstances but by realizing God's presence in the midst of them. Additionally, God becomes the release you long for. David begged, "Bring me out of prison" (v. 7). By "prison" did David mean the cave to which he'd fled? Or was it the confinement of loneliness itself? David, a shepherd, was a man of the open fields. The confinement of the cave must have tormented him. Yet God drew near and delivered him from the confinement of the even more limiting loneliness he felt. Finally, God becomes your reward. David told God, "You are . . . my portion in the land of the living" (v. 5). The word "portion" describes a person's share in an inheritance. David was telling God, "You are all I want in this life" (TEV).

Here's the amazing thing: when we become this satisfied in God alone, He often rewards such solitary faith with other relationships. "The righteous will surround me, for you will deal bountifully with me" (v. 7). What hope! That final word is given special emphasis in the original text, as if David were saying, "You will deal bountifully with *me . . .* even *me . . . me of all people!*"

Amazingly this is precisely what God did for David. In the historical record we read, "And when his brothers and all his father's house heard it, they went down there to him. And everyone who was in distress, and everyone who was in debt, and everyone who was bitter in soul, gathered to him. And he became captain over them. And there were with him about four hundred men" (1 Sam. 22:1–2).

As I studied this psalm a sentence read long ago kept reverberating through my head: "*The route to knowing God eventually passes directly through the valley of profound loneliness.*" It nagged at my mind so incessantly that I finally found the book and looked it up. I found this sentence tagged to it: "It is in the times when there is no one but God that we learn to know Him most fully." It was Larry Crabb who wrote these words as he described the need to look to God alone for the satisfaction of our needs. Halfway down the page I encountered these words:

Sometime ago I was sharing these thoughts with a group of people in another country. After one of my messages, a man in his late twenties approached me with a story he felt impressed to relate. During the previous year, his wife had undergone a double mastectomy because of cancer. From diagnosis through surgery and on to the present, he had struggled to remain strong for his wife, wanting to be a source of encouragement for her. His own pain, confusion, and fear were nearly crippling him emotionally, but he devoted himself to the one purpose of ministering to his wife.

The young man asked me to read Psalm 142 aloud. As I thumbed through my Bible, he told me of the many nights when sleep would not come, nights when—sometimes with his wife, sometimes alone, but always with tears—he would read the words of that psalm in prayer. I found the passage and read these words:

> When my spirit was overwhelmed within me,
> Thou didst know my path (v. 3).
>
> No one cares for my soul.
> I cried out to Thee, O Lord;
> I said, "Thou art my refuge,
> My portion in the land of the living" (vv. 4, 5).
>
> "Give heed to my cry,
> For I am brought very low" (v. 6).
> "Bring my soul out of prison; . . .
> Thou wilt deal bountifully with me" (v. 7).

My voice was unsteady as I read, and my eyes could barely contain the wetness. I realized that I was reading words of life to this young man, words that had been his pathway to deep communion with God.[2]

Praying Through

Linger with God now in prayer. Process through your loneliness, using Psalm 142 as a guide.

- Find a place where you can not only be alone with God, but audible with Him. Lift the cry of your loneliness to God. Speak it. Sound it. Let it go. Make it not only from your heart, but with your voice.

- Speak to God about the overwhelming nature of your loneliness. Describe what feels unjust and unloving about how the people who are in your life treat you. Tell God your feelings of abandonment. Don't rush. Be committed to pray thoroughly through all these emotions.

- Now vocalize your gratitude to God, thanking Him as the only one who knows what you feel and what you face. Write out a prayer to God in which you clearly and confidently take Him to be your refuge, rescue, release and reward. Pray this back to God with the conviction that comes from emerging on the other side of the crushing loneliness. Be committed to repeat this process as often as necessary.

5

Praying Through Atrocity

"**M**URDERED!... Eighty-five priests!... Slaughtered! ... Cut down!"

The disconnected phrases poured out between frantic gasps for air. The wild look in the lad's eyes betrayed the horrifying trauma he'd witnessed. Swords flashed and spears were drawn as he'd come stumbling into the midst of David's camp and had thrown himself at the would-be king's feet. David's men instantly surrounded the intruder.

Despite the show of force the distraught young man continued his disjointed report. "Dead! All of them! Ahimelech, my father, butchered!"

Ahimelech? Suddenly David recognized the boy. "Abiathar, is that you?" he inquired as he dropped to his knees beside him. The lad's head affirmatively bobbed up and down in wild-eyed fright. David gently brushed the boy's hair back from his sweat-streaked face. "It's OK. Slow down. You're safe here."

For a few moments he held the boy as he convulsed for breaths. Eventually he was able to put together coherent sentences. "Saul sent to Nob demanding my father and the other priests appear before him. When we arrived Saul was full into one of his tantrums. He interrogated my fa-

ther about your visit to Nob. My father told him you had
come on official business, requested bread and a weapon
and then were on your way. Saul ranted some nonsense
about his complicity in a conspiracy. And then he, he . . ."
Abiathar struggled to form the words, "he ordered his men
to slaughter my father and our family!"

Abiathar stopped to study David's face. Sensing permission to continue he reported, "The men refused, but
that threw Saul into an even more violent rage." The boy
paused, took a deep breath, swallowed hard and then said,
"Then he said to Doeg, his chief shepherd, 'You turn and
strike the priests!'"

"Doeg," David repeated only half-audibly. He'd heard
enough. The tears that swam over the lad's eyes told the
rest of tale. He could guess how the saga ended. When
pandering meets paranoia the outcome is predictable.[1]

• • • • •

Atrocity—the word dredges up names like Hitler, Amin,
Milosevic, Dahmer and Ceausescu. It comes from a Latin
root meaning cruelty. It describes actions so outrageous,
so morally repugnant, so ethically shocking that all who
hear of them are repulsed.

When I hear the word I think of a place called
Kuropathy. It's the name given to a sad forest of evergreens
just outside the city of Minsk in the country of Belarus.
During my visit the winter winds whispered through the
pines whose boughs sagged low under the weight of snow.
The quiet stillness failed to cover completely the sadness
of the place. Sagging low spots dotted the forest floor,
scarcely hiding the mass graves that lay beneath. During

Stalinist purges of the old Soviet world, Kuropathy had served as a convenient killing field for "enemies of the state" in these regions of the federation. Between 1937 and 1941 they were brought in an average of sixteen truckloads a day, shot and buried in whatever position they fell into the pits dug for their graves. Soldiers brought handguns by the gunnysack-full to complete their day's work. They would fire at a rate that would soon render the pistol too hot to handle. It would be tossed aside and another selected, and immediately the procession continued until it too burned the hands of its owner. Those who helped the state identify undesirables received the equivalent of $150 per head. In tough economic times such "loyalty" to the state became a cottage industry. It put food on the table. No one knows exactly how many thousands perished there. But they say that in Kuropathy "the trees still weep."

> *We live in a world full of atrocities. How are we to process this? What are we to do when the atrocity comes to our home, our family, or our friends?*

We live in a world full of atrocities. Kuropathy has cousins all around the globe. In this age of exponential growth in technology, we are bombarded constantly by the bloody images and descriptive details. How are we to process all of this? Indeed what are we to do when the atrocity comes to our home, our family or our friends?

In the account of David's flight from Saul and stopover in Nob to ask bread and a sword from Ahimelech, what seemed an otherwise insignificant historical detail now serves as an ominous note of atrocity to come: "Now a certain man of the servants of Saul was there that day, detained before the LORD. His name was Doeg the Edomite, the chief of Saul's herdsmen" (1 Sam. 21:7). Sometime later, as David was detained in Gath and escaping to the cave, Doeg saw an opportunity to gain Saul's good graces and reported David's visit to Nob (1 Sam. 22:9–10). Having summoned all the priests of the community to him, Saul first grilled them; then having rejected their testimony, ordered his men to slaughter them. When his own soldiers refused to draw the sword against the innocent priests, "Then the king said to Doeg, 'You turn and strike the priests.' And Doeg the Edomite turned and struck down the priests, and he killed on that day eighty-five persons who wore the linen ephod. And Nob, the city of the priests, he put to the sword; both man and woman, child and infant, ox, donkey and sheep, he put to the sword" (1 Sam. 22:18–19). One can almost see the grizzly scene—an exhausted, but ambitious sheepherder, chest heaving for breaths, blood spattered over every square inch of his body, eyes fixed upon the king, looking for his approval. In the background are piled the disfigured corpses of young and old alike, men and women together. Infants lie dead next to oxen. Flies start to swarm. Scavenger birds begin to circle above.

When David received the news from Ahimelech's son, Abiathar, he turned to God in prayer. The result is Psalm 52, a model of the hard work of praying through atrocity. We should sound here a reminder that praying through does not promise an instant fix for the troubles of life. No predetermined time schedule is implied. Living in an age where every problem raised on television is resolved in sixty minutes or less, we tend to imagine there must be jiffy answers to all our problems. Praying through is not a magic pill. Rather it is the means of putting us in connection with God who sovereignly rules this world—a world which at the moment is full of atrocities, a world He will one day judge, put right, and mete out justice to. Praying through is a process. Breaking through to the fullness of life God promises is the goal. Praying is the means of seeing my heart conformed to God's heart, not wringing from his hands convenient fixes. As I pray through I am the one being changed, not God's mind or will. Such transformation includes seeing accurately the perpetrator of the atrocity.

Psalm 52

To the choirmaster. A Maskil of David, when Doeg, the Edomite, came and told Saul, "David has come to the house of Ahimelech."

> *¹ Why do you boast of evil, O mighty man?*
>   *The steadfast love of God endures all the day.*
> *² Your tongue plots destruction,*
>   *like a sharp razor, you worker of deceit.*
> *³ You love evil more than good,*
>   *and lying more than speaking what is right. Selah*
> *⁴ You love all words that devour,*
>   *O deceitful tongue.*

The Perpetrator of Atrocity

David began by reminding himself who Doeg was before God. In so doing he took note of *the hollow victories of little men.* He prayed, "Why do you boast of evil, O mighty man? The steadfast love of God endures all the day" (v. 1). Read David's designation of Doeg as a "mighty man" with biting sarcasm. The term is one reserved for the most courageous and dominant of military men. Doeg was a sheepherder, not a soldier. He was a wanna-be. David was the true "mighty man." In fact this is the term used when Saul was looking for someone among the soldiers of Israel willing to fight Goliath. The only one to step forward had been youthful, inexperienced David—soon enough Israel knew who the real "mighty man" was (1 Sam. 16:18). David had made the transition from shepherd to mighty man through character and courage. Doeg sought passage by means of intrigue and ambition.

Doeg had seen David face to face in Nob, but did nothing. He waited to act until David was not present and the potential payoff was large enough. The "boast" David accused Doeg of refers not to loud braggadocio, but an inward smug self-satisfaction.

Many of the world's worst atrocities are committed by little men trying to become someone important, from a Hitler trying to overcome his ignominious origins to a Lee Harvey Oswald desperately trying to make the world stand up and notice him. In the climb such people may gain the headlines but will forfeit their soul. The momentary notice is insignificant in comparison to the price paid to obtain it.

David also described *the big talk of little men.* "Your tongue plots destruction, like a sharp razor, you worker of deceit. You love evil more than good, and lying more than speaking what is right. You love words that devour, O deceitful tongue" (vv. 2–4).

Strange, isn't it, that the man who took sword in hand and diced to pieces priests, women, babies, livestock and pets, is the one whose words are likened to razors. Note the character of the words. They are arrogant ("Why do you boast," v. 1), deceptive ("worker of deceit . . . lying . . . deceitful tongue," vv. 2–4) and destructive ("Your tongue plots destruction . . . You love all words that devour," vv. 2, 4).

David also laid bare *the vile character of little men*. Such a man does evil (v. 1), talks evil (vv. 2-4) and loves evil (v. 3). Note the unholy regression. It is one thing to talk of evil, another to do evil, but altogether another thing to *love* evil. There is a dark, downward descent into decadence: doing, talking, loving. How does one get to the place where he commits atrocity? Reverse the order of David's prayer and the answer is clear: it arises from a depraved heart, is betrayed through deviant talk and ultimately issues in despicable action.

How does one get to the place where he commits atrocity? It arises from a depraved heart, is betrayed through deviant talk and ultimately issues in despicable action.

This same order of heart, mouth, action is the one Jesus taught us to watch for: "The good person out of the good treasure of his heart produces good, and the evil person out of his evil treasure produces evil, for out of the abundance of the heart his mouth speaks" (Luke 6:45).

Doeg did not run to inform Saul the moment he spotted David. He savored his tidbit of information. He ruminated upon it. He planned, plotted and premeditated his next move. When the strategic moment was at hand, he shared his news with Saul. Words, and their timing, reveal the character of a person's heart.

What value is found in recounting before God the nature of such despicable individuals? Why not just ignore them and go straight to God and focus upon Him? The answer is that crimes of atrocity are of such a magnitude that their effects simply cannot be ignored or bypassed. To rush past the harsh realities and pretend (even when "sanctified" in prayer) is only to delay the inevitable. We must process the horrors, and we must do it before God. Any perceived gains made without praying through the perpetrator of the atrocity will be short-lived.

If the atrocity hits close to home, your hesitancy here may not be motivated so much by faith as by fear. You don't want to relive the gruesome events. You want to quarantine the images, the violation of your sensibilities and the trauma of your spirit and heart. But no walls exist to contain such pain. The trauma will show up again unless you get this out before God.

David's prayer is an example of naming things as God sees them. God is just; He despises injustice. He is a God of mercy; He deplores the ruthless. He is a God of kindness; He detests brutality and abuse. Our God is the Judge of all the earth. He calls things as they are. He invites us to Himself in order that we might learn to do the same. In the messiness of the trauma, abuse and revulsion, we need our hearts conformed to God's heart. This only takes place in the presence of God as we pray through to resolution regarding the perpetrator of the atrocity. We likely won't arrive there in our first run at praying through. We must linger. We may have to pray again and again. This is not tidy, swift work. It is the re-molding of a heart deformed by scenes and experiences no human heart was designed to witness or live through.

God wants us to see as He sees and speak as He speaks. To do so is to find the deep health and healing our hearts require. To arrive there requires difficult, painful seasons of prayer. It may well require a faithful, mature and experienced friend to pray through with you. But pray we must, until we have broken through to the place where we share a measure of God's heart regarding the perpetrator of the atrocity.

> *5 But God will break you down forever;*
> *he will snatch and tear you from your tent;*
> *he will uproot you from the land of the living. Selah*
> *6 The righteous shall see and fear,*
> *and shall laugh at him, saying,*
> *7 "See the man who would not make God his refuge,*
> *but trusted in the abundance of his riches*
> *and sought refuge in his own destruction!"*

The Penalty for Atrocity

Praying through also means prayerfully embracing the price of the abomination. This may be as difficult for some to do as it is easy for others. The struggle of the latter may be to arrive at the place of *holy* retribution, of *divine* justice. Even if they willingly acknowledge that "We know him who said, 'Vengeance is mine; I will repay'" (Heb. 10:30), they find it hard to stay their hand from bitter revenge and may relish God's judgment upon the violator with ill motive. Others, however, struggle to share God's heart of hatred toward both sin and sinner (Ps. 26:5, 31:6, 139:21–22). Such folks want simply to "move on," refusing to embrace the God of justice.

However the fact is *God will judge*. "God will break you down forever; he will snatch and tear you from your tent; he will uproot you from the land of the living" (v. 5). God's judgment is depicted by means of graphic verbal forms.[2] God's judgment is a bringing down—like an unwanted building's implosion into a pile of useless waste, so the perpetrator will be reduced to rubble by God's hand. As the walls of Jericho fell in upon themselves in God's judgment against its citizens, so the evil one will cave in before God's hand of judgment. God's judgment is also a snatching up. The word was used to describe the taking away of cold ashes from the hearth of a furnace.[3] As a coal of fire snatched from the fire soon burns out, so will the violator stand alone before God and be reduced to a has-been. God's judgment is also a tearing away—"he will snatch and tear you from your tent." In the midst of apparent security and success, God will suddenly rip the ungodly from his sleep. Finally the judgment of God is pictured as an uprooting. The perpetrator's undoing is pictured in vivid terms—bringing down, snatching up, tearing away and uprooting "from the land of the living." Unlike the godly for whom "the root of the righteous will never be moved" (Prov. 12:3), the ungodly will be snatched up root and all at a time they do not expect.

Such vivid images, and the powerful divine judgment they represent, can be difficult to make your own in prayer. Many Christians struggle to join God in condemning even the worst of human atrocities and those who commit them. Too often we take a weak, spineless response—thinking that being people of grace requires never being people of justice. We must pray through, always being ready to extend grace but never backing away from sharing God's heart of justice.

There is coming a day when *the righteous will mock*. "The righteous shall see and fear, and shall laugh at him, saying, 'See the man who would not make God his refuge, but trusted in the abundance of his riches and sought refuge in his own destruction'" (vv. 6, 7). David's prayer is filled with biting scorn for Doeg— from sarcastically designating him a "mighty man" (v. 1) to the laughter that the righteous will join in over his fallen corpse (v. 6). The intimidation they employed to cause others to respect them will backfire, and the righteous, seeing the outcome of such atrocities, will fear the Lord (v. 6).

> *As we pray through atrocity, we must always be ready to extend grace without backing away from sharing God's heart of justice.*

Once again, it is well nigh impossible for redeemed, but as yet not glorified, people to share perfectly with the Lord in such derision. But praying through atrocity requires in some measure sharing God's heart with Him, even in retribution and judgment. God will mock those who have rejected the fear of the Lord (Prov. 1:26–27). While never pronouncing ultimate judgment, we must anticipate that outcome against the wickedness we both witness and experience at the hands of others. This re-

quires thorough prayer—praying through to the place
where such a response grows not out of bitter, personal
vengeance but from a holy concern for the righteous character of God. Praying through to such a place will likely
not be quick and easy.

> *⁸ But I am like a green olive tree*
>   *in the house of God.*
> *I trust in the steadfast love of God*
>   *forever and ever.*
> *⁹ I will thank you forever,*
>   *because you have done it.*
> *I will wait for your name, for it is good,*
>   *in the presence of the godly.*

This most difficult of prayers, however, finishes on a
note of hope. David reminded himself and God that *the
faithful will be vindicated.* "But I am like a green olive tree in
the house of God. I trust in the steadfast love of God forever and ever. I will thank you forever, because you have
done it. I will wait for your name, for it is good, in the
presence of the godly" (vv. 8–9).

The olive tree was a picture of vitality and enduring
life. An olive tree may live for hundreds of years. The
metaphor stands in stark contrast to him who will be uprooted and snatched away while in the midst of apparent
security and success (v. 5). David's ongoing "trust in the
steadfast love of God" (v. 8) stands in direct contrast to
that of Doeg who "trusted in the abundance of his riches"
(v. 7). Trust that endures "forever and ever" (v. 8) becomes
a heart of praise that endures "forever" (v. 9). The moment may have belonged to the wicked, but time is on the

side of the righteous. In the end one will flourish even while the other withers, uprooted and cast aside.

There is a day of reckoning coming—a day when God will judge, the righteous will join Him in holy scorn and the faithful will be vindicated for their enduring trust in God. That day *is* coming. Pray through till you believe it with all your heart.

But in a world of constant atrocities, how do we pray through to that day? We must embrace the justice of God, not merely in theory but in the specifics of a world of atrocities. Yet we must pray through to the place where the "steadfast love of God" is most central before our eyes—not the atrocity, nor its perpetrator and not even God's judgment on him. We must pray through and avoid being mired in vengeance. We must emerge on the other side of atrocity into a place of hope. Because David did so we are able to confidently pray through to the same hope.

René Bousquet was responsible, as the chief of police for France's Vichy government, for sending over 60,000 Jews, including 3,500 children, to Nazi death camps during World War II. Following the war Bousquet went unpunished and remained apparently unrepentant for nearly fifty years. He became a dignified banker, living a Parisian life of well-heeled luxury. A half-century too late Nazi hunter Serge Klarsfeld finally convinced French officials to open a case against Bousquet, and the trial for the infamous Nazi collaborator was set to open in September 1993.

René Bousquet, however, never made it to court. Just a few weeks before the trial date, a frustrated novelist by the name of Christian Didier rang the bell at Bousquet's Paris apartment and, when he opened the door, gunned the 84-

year-old down with four shots to the chest from point blank range. Both French citizens and the Jewish community were robbed of the opportunity for the justice they deserved. When asked why he had killed Bousquet, Didier replied only, "I was good and he was evil."[4]

Was Didier correct? Was he good and Bousquet evil? In a world of atrocities it is nearly impossible to so neatly divide up the horrors and assign blame and praise. Bousquet was unquestionably evil. Didier's actions were also evil. In a world of atrocities it can be a short slide from abused to abuser. In the face of unspeakable horror, some question how anyone can continue in faith and prayer. The answer is simple: praying through in faith is the only assurance that we will not multiply the atrocity by committing another ourselves. Only praying through atrocity to the place of restful hope assures we will stay off of the slippery slide that would take us to ruin unspeakable.

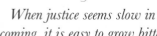

When justice seems slow in coming, it is easy to grow bitter and impatient. Do we really believe God will bring a day of reckoning and judgment?

When justice seems slow in coming, it is easy to grow bitter and impatient. It is in such times when we prove the reality of whether or not we believe God will indeed bring a day of reckoning and judgment. How does such faith evidence itself? By praying through to hope. James Montgomery Boice suggests, from David's prayer, three evidences that we are in the process of truly praying through the atrocities of life.[5] Ask yourself: Am I worshiping God (v. 9)? Am I trusting in God (v. 8)? Am I witnessing of this hope in God (v. 9)?

Praying Through

Praying through such deep trauma will take time. Schedule some time now to be alone with God. You will likely need a trusted, mature friend who is willing to pray and process through this with you.

- As you begin, describe to God in detail the atrocity you have been a victim of or a witness to. Don't rush. God knows the details, but you need to lance the boil of bitterness that has festered in isolation.

- Join God in denouncing the person who brought this pain upon you or others. Put them in proper perspective before God. Do not hesitate to call their actions and character what they are.

- Now entrust judgment of this person to God. Tell Him you are leaving to Him the work of bringing down, snatching up, tearing away and uprooting this person. Covenant with God that you will not take personal vengeance upon the person. Take them off your hook and put them on God's hook. They are His responsibility. Pray through until that is true in your heart.

- Pray through to the place where you can genuinely entrust the person and their judgment to God. Pray through until you can take up the hope of God's steadfast love for your future. Pray through until you can genuinely praise God with liberty in your heart, trusting Him to be the sovereign God who will do right in all the earth and in your particular trauma.

6

Praying Through Treachery

A CLOUD of dust ascended from the cliff-sides as hundreds of mercenaries scrambled about frantically, snatching up weaponry, half-eaten loaves of bread and clothing laid out to dry on the rocks. The sentry's alarm had landed them all upon their feet, but it was the winded messenger's warning that sent them into motion: "The Ziphites have betrayed you! Saul is on the other side of the mountain!"

As his men crammed their treasures into hastily packed rucksacks and snuffed out their smoldering campfires, the anointed one sat in dazed stillness, unfazed by the frenetic scurrying about him. While the news sent adrenaline pumping through their veins, it seemed to stun their leader. All the synonyms tumbled through David's mind without conscious effort or notice: Snitch. Traitor. Double-crosser. Stool pigeon. Squealer. Informant. Turncoat. Betrayer. Family.

Wait!

David raised his head, fixing his gaze upon some indefinite point across the vast lowlands that lay before him. His focus, however, was not upon the landscape, it was on that last word. It turned over again uneasily in his mind:

family. Finally the question formed in his mind, *How could they?* Had he not just risked everything by leaving his desert hideout and going to the rescue of his brothers in Keilah? Again the question came like a bullet train out of a dense fog, *How could they?* And right behind it came its corollary, *Why would they?*

Just then a calloused hand fastened around David's wrist and, respectfully but firmly, yanked him down the path behind the several hundred frantic soldiers. They tumbled along the narrow ridges and scurried hastily over rocky escarpments, all the while casting wary glances over their shoulders, searching the hillside for signs of Saul's army.

The eagle motionlessly riding the updrafts hundreds of feet above them curiously watched the sad comedy unfolding below—Saul's vast army on one side of the mountain and David's militia on the other, each in a full-throttled right-hand turn around the mountain. The outcome lay in the answer to who would either fall or fatigue first. Saul's greater numbers put the odds squarely in his favor. As his men gained ground on David's band, the eagle continued to trace their motion in the sky.

His army, however, was not the only thing going in circles; David's thoughts were as well. And those simple but searching words led the way: *family—why?*[1]

· · · · ·

Your spouse is found in the arms of another. Your partners are caught conspiring against you. Your siblings lobby Mom and Dad to exclude you from the will. When bonds that are meant to last are broken, it renders us nearly incapable of ever trusting again. At such moments it is difficult even to pray, let alone pray through to a place of resolution and release.

Ask David—he experienced more than his share of treachery. Psalm 54 finds him back at the hard work of praying through the pain of a broken trust. The historical account behind this prayer paints a vivid picture of treachery. David had received word that the Philistines were looting the Judean village of Keilah. "Go and attack the Philistines and save Keilah," was God's command (1 Sam. 23:2). After initial hesitation from his men and God's reconfirmation of this divine authorization for the operation, David and his army rose and drove the Philistines away.

No sooner had David delivered the people of Keilah than he received word that Saul knew of his presence there and was coming to kill him. He turned to Abiathar, the now-orphaned son of Ahimelech the priest. As he fled the slaughter of priests in Nob, Abiathar had grabbed the holy ephod. By means of the *Urim* and *Thummim* he inquired of God on David's behalf: "Will the men of Keilah surrender me into his hand?" God's simple answer: "They will surrender you" (v. 12). Grimacing from the sting of

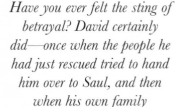

Have you ever felt the sting of betrayal? David certainly did—once when the people he had just rescued tried to hand him over to Saul, and then when his own family sold him out!

treachery's blade in his back, David fled with his men deeper into his home territory of Judah to the wilderness of Ziph.

And then David received a second knife in the back—the Ziphites also betrayed David to the king! One wonders why. Perhaps it was out of fear that Saul would visit their village with a slaughter as he did to Nob. Maybe it was an opportunistic ploy for prominence. Whatever the motive they sent this message to the king: "Is not David hiding among us in the strongholds at Horesh . . . ? Now come down, O king, according to all your heart's desire to come down, and our part shall be to surrender him into the king's hand" (vv. 19–20).

The king's response? "May you be blessed of the LORD" (v. 21). Note the misplaced and manipulated spirituality! Then Saul recruited the Ziphites to bring him even more certain intelligence. As they launched on their royal commission, Saul shouted out after them, "I will search him out among all the thousands of Judah" (v. 23). Not even his own family would protect David.

Psalm 54

To the choirmaster: with stringed instruments. A Maskil of David, when the Ziphites went and told Saul, "Is not David hiding among us?"

> *¹ O God, save me, by your name,*
> *and vindicate me by your might.*
> *² O God, hear my prayer;*
> *give ear to the words of my mouth.*
> *³ For strangers have risen against me;*
> *ruthless men seek my life;*
> *they do not set God before themselves. Selah*

The Ziphites twisted the knife the people of Keilah had already buried in David's back. Not even his kinsmen would stand with him. Indeed his fellow tribesmen were behaving like unbelieving "strangers" (v. 3).[2] They were "ruthless men" (v. 3) who, rather than behaving like family, had become his "enemies" (v. 5). There is no place like home—but when family sells you out, no place is safe.

Just as Saul's hand was about to lay hold of David's throat, he was providentially called away to deal with a raid by the Philistines (1 Sam. 23:27–28). The Philistines that had been the raiding bullies in Keilah (v. 1) had now become the pawns of God deployed to deliver His anointed (vv. 27-29). As the dust settled and David found a new cave to hide in (v. 29), treachery's gaping wound oozed blood-red and raw. David should have considered himself blessed to have breath left in his lungs. He was more concerned how he could use it now to pray through the pain inflicted by those he should have been able to trust.

Know the feeling? I'll bet you do. Psalm 54 is the result of David's resilient refusal to let go of God. He was determined to pray through wave after wave of betrayal. But prayer is supremely an act of trust. So how do you pray when you've just been sold out by those you should have been able to trust the most? God, of course, did not let David down. But the pain of betrayal does not discriminate when it clamps down on the throat of prayer. What moves us at such moments to pray again?

Prayer is supremely an act of trust. So how do you pray when you've just been sold out by those you should have been able to trust the most?

The Name of God

For David it was the knowledge of the name of God that moved him to dare to speak it once again in prayer. Hear David's first breath: "O God, save me, by your name, and vindicate me by your might" (v. 1). Why did he ask for deliverance by means of the "name" of God? Why not His faithfulness? Or power? Or holiness or wisdom?

Names, for us, are merely the means of identifying who we are. Some parents choose their child's name because they want to honor a parent. Others strive for balance and rhythm in syllables. Some aim for a rhyming sound. Still others choose names that are popular at the time. Not so the Hebrews. They believed a person's name revealed the quality or character of the one it designated. It was an outward indicator of an inward, unseen substance. Walter Kaiser believes that to the Hebrews the word comes closer than any other to what we mean by personality.[3] In short a name was revelatory. This was never more true than with God. Indeed the name of God is a summation of His entire self-disclosure.[4]

When David was betrayed by all, and the wound in his back was still searing, he went back to the one unchanging Rock. David's son Solomon would later write, "The name of the LORD is a strong tower; the righteous man runs into it and is safe" (Prov. 18:10). He must have studied his father's prayer life. David began his prayer with God's name (v. 1) and he ended on the same theme:

> [6] *With a freewill offering I will sacrifice to you;*
> *I will give thanks to your name, O LORD, for it is good.*

Three names of God became audible in David's cry. He called him "God" (vv. 1–4), the Hebrew *Elohim*. This was the name especially used in the creation account. It stresses God's great power. G. Campbell Morgan says the name emphasizes God's "absolute, unqualified, unlimited energy." This is why David paired a plea for salvation by God's "name" with a request for deliverance by his "might" (v. 1). David probably began with this name because he was outnumbered, surrounded and betrayed. Power was his problem, so he looked to the One who possesses all power.

Next David called out to "the Lord." The name is *Adonai*. "Behold, God is my helper; the Lord is the upholder of my life" (v. 4). While *Elohim* stresses God's power, *Adonai* recognizes Him as Sovereign and King. *Adonai* is Master. David admitted that his life was not his own. He was a man under authority and on a divine commission. It was not ultimately in his hands to keep his own life. The One who called and anointed him was "the upholder of [his] life."

Finally, David called out to the "LORD." The Hebrew name is *Yahweh*. "I will give thanks to your name, O LORD, for it is good" (v. 6). The name *Yahweh* is beyond description. Scribes so feared the name that they could not bring themselves to write it. They used the consonants of this name, but affixed the vowel points of *Adonai*, lest they make a mistake and dishonor the holy name of God.[5] When Moses asked God who he should tell the enslaved Israelites had sent him, God simply replied, "I AM WHO I AM" (Exodus 3:14). The name *Yahweh* comes from the Hebrew verb for "I am."

Yahweh points to God as timeless (I am—eternally present). It designates God as self-existent, thus indicating that He depends upon nothing for His existence. Nothing threatens God. It also points to God's self-sufficiency. God needs nothing. No one supplies Him. He waits on no one. *Yahweh* is the covenant name of God, emphasizing His unfailing promises to His people.

Why do you suppose David closed his prayer with this name on his lips? Because when you've been betrayed by those you trusted the most, your only consolation is Him who is incapable of unfaithfulness and whose promise is sealed by the signet of His eternal character.

> ⁶ *With a freewill offering I will sacrifice to you;*
>   *I will give thanks to your name, O LORD, for it is good.*
> ⁷ *For he has delivered me from every trouble,*
>   *and my eye has looked in triumph on my enemies.*

With the last breath of this prayer David said, "For he has delivered me from every trouble" (v. 7). The "he" is literally "it": "I will give thanks to your name, O LORD, for it is good. For *it* [the name of God] has delivered me from every trouble" (vv. 6–7).[6]

David described his fellow-tribesmen as they who "do not set God before themselves" (v. 3). The same verb is used to describe Doeg's problem in the psalm preceding this one chronologically.[7] What the opportunistic Gentile had been, so David's own kinsman were now. His own family sold him out to the highest bidder. When it suited them for David to rescue them, fine. When it paid better to back Saul, all the better. Unlike the unchanging, solid

rock of God's character, these men of Judah were "oppor-
tunists, standing for no principle, suiting their colour and
shape to the moment."[8]

God's name, however, en-
dures forever—unchanging
and immutable. David, for
his part, had long since determined, "I have set the
Lord always before me" (Ps.
16:8). Because he had set
God before him, he could be

*Because David had set God
before him, he could be confident that God could be trusted
with his back—a back
that bore the scars of
earth's failed trust.*

confident that God could be trusted with his back—a back
that bore the scars of earth's failed trust.

The Titles of God

As powerful as the name of God was to David, he became even more personal in his prayer. This God of all
power, complete independence and unlimited faithfulness
was David's God. David employed not just formal names
for God but personally given titles. Such titles lay bare a
profound intimacy. They arise from shared experiences,
past deliverances and personal encounters with the living
God. Somewhere in each title the word "my" is found—
showing how personally God had ministered to David and
how intimately he had come to cherish God.

I have a friend named Steve. Not long after I met Steve,
I found that those who had known him from youth often
called him Merle. I was confused. Finally I asked what it
was all about. Despite repeated explanations I still don't
get it. I wasn't there. It arose from their high school years

together. I wasn't there, so I just can't understand. Guess you had to be there!

Just so there are some titles you can call God only out of personal encounter and experience. Thus David prayed, "God is my helper" (v. 4). The word refers to one who provides support to another, particularly support of a military nature. When it seemed that David stood alone, God was at his side—and indeed it was in those times that David discovered he was never alone.

This was more than a nickname. There was something more than metaphorical about the title "my helper." Remember, David had approximately 600 men who had affixed themselves to him as his personal army. He was being tracked by the armies of Israel. He had recently defeated the Philistine forces at Keilah. In frighteningly physical and militaristic circumstances, God had been the difference between death and deliverance.

Ask yourself, how does someone get the title "helper"? It doesn't come through phone conversations and long-distance consultations. It comes by showing up on location, pitching in and sharing the load. A person becomes my "helper" by enabling me to do things I could not otherwise do. When I was expanding our boy's room, I had two men who came and helped me with the electrical and drywall. I say they "helped," but the fact is they did it for me while I carried their supplies and ran errands for them. I could not have done it without them. They couldn't have done what they did through email. They showed up, crawled up in a dusty attic, breathed in the insulation, gave of their time and got dirt under their nails. Each was proved to be "my helper."

God longs to be just as personal and immediate to you, even as your recent betrayal tempts you to never allow anyone that close again. Praying through means refusing to say the final "Amen" until you have sufficiently let go of the pain of betrayal and are able to be vulnerable again with God. Through the pain David found God to be present—tangibly and specifically intervening in life's mess. He is ready to be just as present for you.

David also called God "the upholder of my life" (v. 4). The word "upholder" means primarily "to lean upon." It comes also to describe the hand of one who upholds you. The picture in my mind is the injured athlete limping off the field of competition with both arms around teammates and a limp leg hanging uselessly in the air. In his injury and weakness someone upholds him.

In another place David uses the same word to say, "the arms of the wicked shall be broken, but the LORD upholds the righteous" (Ps. 37:17). Indeed God upholds His people by His power (Ps. 37:24) and word (Ps. 119:116).

Imagine for a moment just how exhausted David must have been. He has twice dodged the spear of Saul, escaped his home while surrounded by Saul's henchmen, fled to Nob, on to Gath, pretended to be insane, made a harrowing escape to the cave of Adullum, cried out to God in utter isolation, organized the ragtag mercenaries who gathered around him into an elite military force, shuttled his parents to safety in Moab, scurried from one location to another throughout Judah while staying one step ahead of Saul, learned of the slaughter of the priests in Nob, rescued the city of Keilah, was betrayed by its citizens and later by those of Ziph and now had fled to the

wilderness of Maon and was chased around the mountain, only narrowly escaping death by the providential hand
of God. He needed someone to uphold him! Take a moment or two and tally up the things that have taxed you of
late.

In that great celebration of the Word of God, the psalmist prayed "*Uphold* me according to your promise, that I
may live" (Ps. 119:116). Praying through treachery requires
fighting off the cynicism that crusts over one's heart after betrayal. It means staying doggedly in pursuit of God until His promises form with conviction on our lips and we can hold them with confidence before Him again in prayer. It is exhausting, taxing work. The fainthearted will never stay the course. Lay hold of a promise and refuse to give up until it is yours in experience.

> *Praying through treachery means fighting the cynicism that comes after betrayal. It means doggedly pursuing God until His promises form with conviction on our lips in prayer.*

> ⁴ *Behold, God is my helper;*
> *the Lord is the upholder of my life.*
> ⁵ *He will return the evil to my enemies;*
> *in your faithfulness put an end to them.*

The Acts of God

With the character of God set squarely before the eyes
of his heart and with his faith firmly set on the certainty
that God would personalize His ministry to him, David
prayed for God to act on his behalf. He asked God to "save"

and "vindicate" him (v. 1), to "hear" and "give ear" to his cry (v. 2) and to "put an end" to those who have betrayed him (v. 5). This was, David demanded, a matter of God upholding His own character—"*in your faithfulness* put an end to them" (v. 5).

It is not unimportant that it was only after David had first set God squarely before himself in praise of His names and titles that he was able to make such bold requests. The boldness of our petitions swing on the hinge of our praises. Tozer was correct: "Were we able to extract from any man a complete answer to the question, 'What comes into your mind when you think about God?' we might predict with certainty the spiritual future of that man."[9] If we could determine exactly what a person thinks of God, I also believe we could accurately predict the likelihood that the individual will pray through and emerge into the life God offers them.

What have you recently requested God to do on your behalf? Praying "big prayers" may be nothing more than spiritual bluster and sanctimonious verbosity. We can take up grand superlatives, conveying the impression of great faith, and all the while never really believe God for anything. It is no less sad to pray puny prayers that betray a pathetic view of a paltry god. We can talk at God without knowing His promises or ever truly recounting His character. If you could calculate who you believe God really is and what the certainty of His promises are, you would be able to chart the trajectory of your prayers. It would become immediately apparent whether your prayers would aim high enough to enable you to pray through the thicket of treachery.

David knew God. He knew His name; he had seen Him act. Because he had, despite his pain, he simply could not fail to pray through and emerge into the life God offered him. Such praying brings us inevitably back to the place of confident, committed worship: "With a freewill offering I will sacrifice to you; I will give thanks to your name, O LORD, for it is good. For he has delivered me from every trouble, and my eye has looked in triumph on my enemies" (vv. 6–7). David has prayed through to the place where he is once again certain that God will act on his behalf— indeed it is as good as done ("he has delivered me"). David's confidence in God's action feeds a revived commitment to worship ("I will sacrifice . . . I will give thanks"). The sun of hopefulness has broken through the low, gray clouds of treachery.

Remarkable! Praise while in pain is simply not human. How can we pray through to a place of praise once again? The answer lies in the center of the psalm. Verse 4 functions as a fulcrum upon which we gain the leverage to displace the pain of treachery: "Behold, God is my helper; the Lord is the upholder of my life." Upon this affirmation of trust teeters the difference between a simple prayer for deliverance (vv. 1–3) and the resolution of that prayer in praise for its anticipated realization (vv. 5–7).[10] We must not miss the essential nature of this pivotal confession of faith. Nor dare we miss how David once again found the courage to rest his weight upon God.

The key lies in the historical record of First Samuel 23. Sandwiched between the betrayal of the people of Keilah (vv. 1–14) and the treachery of the Ziphites (vv. 19–29) lies a telling encounter between David and Saul's son Jonathan

(vv. 15–18). Let me reproduce it here so we don't miss its power.

> And Saul sought him every day, but God did not give him into his hand. David saw that Saul had come out to seek his life. David was in the Wilderness of Ziph at Horesh. And Jonathan, Saul's son, rose and went to David at Horesh, and strengthened his hand in God. And he said to him, "Do not fear, for the hand of Saul my father shall not find you. You shall be king over Israel, and I shall be next to you. Saul my father also knows this." And the two of them made a covenant before the Lord. David remained at Horesh, and Jonathan went home. (vv. 14–18)

Though Saul "sought him every day," he was kept from David by God's own hand. While Saul searched in vain for David, Jonathan was readily able to locate him. When he found him he "strengthened his hand in God" (v. 16). That simple phrase veils what must have been an intimate and deeply spiritual interchange between these two friends. We do not know exactly what Jonathan said, nor how long it took before he prevailed and David once again took his hope in God. We are given some idea by the words that are recorded next: "Do not fear, for the hand of Saul my father shall not find you. You shall be king over Israel, and I shall be next to you" (v. 17). This could be nothing more than a renewal of their covenant of friendship made previously (1 Sam. 20).

It is more likely, however, that this is an even deeper, more sweeping covenant. Note again the importance of the pronouns: "*You* shall be king over Israel, and *I* shall be next to you." Jonathan would have been the rightful heir to the throne, but he knew the anointing of God rested upon David. And he upheld it, to the end, even in the face of his own father's fury. Jonathan "strengthened [David's] hand in God" by taking him back to the promise of God.

In the same way Jonathan encouraged David, Jesus comes to us in our lowest moments and reminds us of His promises. He strengthens our hand in God.

He affirmed that God's word was His will and that it would indeed come to pass. It was this very hope that then rose up in fresh faith as David prayed through the treachery of the Ziphites. What the historian records as simply "he strengthened his hand in God" became in David's mouth "Behold, God is my helper; the Lord is the upholder of my life."

The arrangement of First Samuel 23 is no accident—Jonathan's encouragement regarding the promises of God is placed purposefully between the betrayal of Keilah and the treachery of Ziph. David found those he had rescued to be unreliable. He would soon find those of his own tribe to be treacherous. Yet it was the son of Saul himself who set David's heart in confidence upon God and His promises! Dale Ralph Davis helps us draw appropriate and powerful application:

> Some questions we can't answer are yet worth asking. Without Jonathan's ministry to David would the Ziphite betrayal (vv. 19-24) have been more than David could bear? Would treachery (Ziph) on the heels of disillusionment

(Keilah) have proven too much? . . . How necessary to have the faithful one standing amid the infidelities of life.

Perhaps believers cannot help seeing here in Jonathan's mission the shadow of a greater than Jonathan.[11]

Indeed Donald Cole says, "It's as if God is saying, yes, the Ziphites are going to betray you, but you have a friend who sticks closer than a brother, and he is the king's own son."[12] We too have such a friend. He is the King's own Son. While He is the one who reigns, He does come to us in our lowest moments and reminds us of the promises made by the King with regard to our future. He reminds us that we can one day reign with Him. He too strengthens our hand in God when without such encouragement we would likely never find the courage to pray through the treacheries and betrayals of this life.

Such a Friend is our only hope when human relationships prove unreliable. Pray through till you hear His voice again through the pages of Scripture, lifting its promises and affixing them to your heart with fresh faith.

Praying Through

Before you move on from this study, take the time necessary to pray through the treachery that may have come your way. Use Psalm 54 as your guide.

- Run to the strong tower of God's name (Prov. 18:10) through praise. Dwell there. Don't rush. Reflect on God's names. Call on His name. Recount to God what His name means. Describe the person God's names reveal Him to be. Pray through till your feet are set on the rock of God's character and you are certain and confident in His faithfulness.

- Look back over the course of your walk with God. Remember before Him the times He has proven to be your helper. Rehearse the times He has upheld you. Remind yourself before God how faithful He has proven to be. Tell Him you know He will be nothing less for you now, even in this fresh pain of treachery.

- Continue to pray through until Jesus has "strengthened [your] hand in God." Find and tenaciously cling to a particular promise of God made to you in His Word. Linger with God until you know in your heart that promise is true and certain.

- Now turn to God in confident thanks for the deliverance He will bring to you. Put assurance in your voice as you claim the promise in specific fulfillment for your circumstances. Pray through, knowing that Jesus draws near and guarantees the verity of His Word.

7

Praying Through Vengeance

DAVID SHIFTED side to side, trying to tuck the edges of his extra-tunic-turned-blanket around his shoulders. The cave's cool, acrid air sunk into his bones as he lay with eyes opened into the darkness above him. *These caves aren't that bad,* David thought to himself as he blinked away the dry sting in his eyes. He listened to the deep, rhythmic breathing of the sleeping soldiers around him. He thought about his wife Michal. He mused on the previous months on the run. Somehow the panic of it all wasn't as intense. A person can only live at full tension so long. An adrenalin rush can't last forever. *Am I more at peace or have I just "bottomed out" emotionally?* David tossed the question about in the darkness.

Out of the dark a heavy, calloused hand from an unseen figure pressed down over David's mouth while another found its way around his wrist as he instinctively groped for his sword in the darkness. As his eyes bulged in terror and that familiar spike in emotion surged through his body, the hushed whisper of a familiar voice said, "Sir, do not move. Saul and his men are just outside the cave." The hand lifted from his face and his arm was set free. He lay motionless, except to raise his head toward the mouth of the cave. The murmur of approaching voices crawled across the still air.

One by one the sleeping warriors received the word. The strict discipline of David's training and the sheer terror of the moment held them all fast in their places. Hundreds of eyes stared through the darkness at the point of light that flooded through the cave's opening. Suddenly a singular figure silhouetted itself against the bright dawn outside. The figure seemed to speak in authoritative tones to others gathered beyond viewing. Breaths grew shallow and quick as the man turned and entered the cave. Suddenly David recognized the profile and the voice's familiar lilt registered—*It's Saul!*

The utter stillness of the cave did not betray the presence of hundreds of soldiers laying in the darkness. Eyes grew wide and jaws dropped as together they beheld a site they could scarcely believe—the figure turned, faced the mouth of the cave, pulled up his tunic and descended into a familiar but unflattering squat.

The silence of hundreds of suppressed snickers filled the cave. As Saul went about his royal business, one of David's most trusted advisors leaned over, cupped his hands around his mouth and pressed them against David's ear. "This is your day. Let me deliver him into your hands." With a swift, silencing gesture David put to rest his loyal friend's plan.

But David had to admit there was something deeply satisfying in the thought. The words reverberated in his mind: "This is your day." *It's about time*, he thought to himself.

David paused, then, without looking, slipped his hand around the butt of his knife. Gently he placed the blade between his teeth, got on all fours and began a daring, silent prowl not unlike the lions that had once hunted his sheep. His men watched in glee has he descended slowly, silently upon his unsuspecting and preoccupied prey.[1]

•   •   •   •   •

Larry Fuller stepped out into a clear, seventy-degree Texas day and soaked in the late October sun. The warmth of the sun he had not felt for so long could not match the gratitude rising in his heart—he was a free man. Twenty-five years after a wrongful conviction for aggravated rape, Larry Fuller finally stepped out of the prison that had unwillingly become his home for nearly half his life. Fuller was a decorated Vietnam veteran in 1981 when a jury convicted and sentenced him to fifty years behind bars. But while Larry languished in a cell, beyond the walls others labored to obtain the DNA testing they believed would reveal the truth. Eventually they got their wish. Now Larry Fuller is once again a free man. But over 9,000 days of his life were taken from him by a flawed judicial system. His response upon being freed? "There's no bitterness," he said. "This is what life is about—trial and tribulation."[2]

No! That can't be the end of the story. That's unjust. No one can be robbed of half his life and not be bitter. Somebody's got to pay! There must be justice!

Any soul beleaguered by injustice knows the overwhelming desire to be vindictive. Yet vengeance is an odd emotion. You take it up only because you think it will devour your wrongdoer. In the end it consumes you.

There is another way. Jesus made it clear. Of him Isaiah

prophesied, "He was oppressed, and he was afflicted, yet he opened not his mouth; like a lamb led to the slaughter, and like a sheep that before its shearers is silent, so he opened not his mouth" (Isa. 53:7). William Temple reminded us, "We are called to the hardest of tasks: to fight without hatred, to resist without bitterness, and in the end if God grant it so, to triumph without vindictiveness."

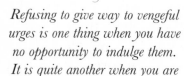

Refusing to give way to vengeful urges is one thing when you have no opportunity to indulge them. It is quite another when you are handed a prime opportunity for payback.

David wrestled time and again with the urge to exact vengeance upon his enemies, particularly Saul. Yet somehow he consistently rejected attempts at self-vindication. Refusing to give way to vengeful urges is one thing when you have no opportunity to indulge them. It is quite another when you are handed a prime opportunity for payback. You are tempted even to call it providence, justice or an open door.

Such an opportunity was set before David just before he penned Psalm 57. While Saul was hunting David in the rugged Engedi region, the king stepped aside into a cave "to relieve himself" (1 Sam. 24:3).[3] Little did he know that David and his men were hiding in the cave. Not only did he not know he was embarrassing himself, Saul was oblivious to the danger he'd placed himself in. David's men urged him to slay his pursuer, insisting it was God's doing (v. 4). David "arose and stealthily cut off a corner of Saul's robe" (v. 5). He did not slay Saul, but he proved he could have. Later, outside the cave and from a safe distance, David showed Saul the piece of cloth he'd cut from

his robe. Saul, stricken of heart, momentarily turned back
from his pursuit.

Psalm 57

To the choirmaster: according to Do Not Destroy.
A Miktam of David, when he fled from Saul, in the cave.

¹ Be merciful to me, O God, be merciful to me,
*   for in you my soul takes refuge;*
in the shadow of your wings I will take refuge,
*   till the storms of destruction pass by.*
² I cry out to God Most High,
*   to God who fulfills his purpose for me.*

Knife in hand and Saul's throat laid bare—how did
David resist the gravitational pull of vengeance? His sub-
sequent prayer reveals the key. As self-vindication began
to reel in David, he prayed, "I cry out . . . to God who
fulfills his purpose for me" (v. 2). See it? Try again, noting
the emphasis: "who fulfills *his purpose* for me." His purpose—have I bound myself to it? When the seemingly ir-
resistible undertow of vengeance begins to draw me downward, only the tether of God's purpose can hold me firm.
David had long since ceased to live for his own purposes.
He was anointed of God. His life was no longer his own.
His wishes, desires and demands did not control his actions. It can be no different for us. We must pray through
until God's purpose is unquestionably our own. Along this
pathway no light entreaties or trite prayers will suffice. The
bloody work of excising selfish purposes from our hearts
and transplanting God's in their place requires stamina
and fortitude.

My Enemies

Praying through begins with honestly assessing those you wish to exact vengeance upon. Too often wishful thinking takes the place of honest praying. Believing the best can be an evidence of grace (1 Cor. 13:7) but avoiding the facts is often an indicator of weakness. David resolutely refused to call Saul an enemy,[4] yet he was honest about his aims and actions. The pressure of polite-but-dishonest-Christianity makes for pretentious praying. Such prayers only perpetuate the status quo.

> [4] *My soul is in the midst of lions;*
> *I lie down amid fiery beasts—*
> *the children of man, whose teeth are spears and arrows,*
> *whose tongues are sharp swords.*

> [5] *Be exalted, O God, above the heavens!*
> *Let your glory be over all the earth!*

Like David we must admit that sometimes our enemies seem like *beasts who surround us.* "My soul is in the midst of lions; I lie down amid fiery beasts" (v. 4). The lion is well named the King of Beasts. Its overwhelming power and disabling intimidation make it one of David's more frequent images in the Psalms.[5] David had fallen "in the midst" of the lions' lair and was made to "lie down" in the middle of their hungry brood. Every hiding place David could find was in the midst of Saul's kingdom. He was surrounded. The deep guttural rumble of the lions' throaty growls surrounded him. Their eyes had fixed upon his frozen frame. He could feel their hot breath in his face. I wonder if many years later in Babylon Daniel took up David's prayer after King Darius dropped him into the lion's den!

We've been there emotionally. We appear to be at the mercy of those with the power of rumor, position or political influence. Their appetite seems to be the only power at play, their wish the only will at issue. It feels like that, and unless we pray through the feelings, we will never break out of the grip of vengeance. There are moments when we want to cry over our own lives as Darius did over Daniel's— "O Daniel, servant of the liv-

Faith says that God will deliver us from our enemies, but we must pray through the contrary feelings on the way to such faith.

ing God, has your God, whom you serve continually, been able to deliver you from the lions?" (Dan. 6:20). Faith says that the issue was never in doubt, but we must pray through the contrary feelings on the way to such faith.

Sometimes our enemies also appear as *soldiers who attack us*. It seems their "teeth are spears and arrows" and their "tongues are sharp swords" (v. 4). Spears, arrows and swords have but one purpose in the hand of a trained soldier—death of an enemy. In this case their speech ("teeth," "tongues") is the weapon of choice. Another king later observed, "There are those whose teeth are swords, whose fangs are knives, to devour the poor from off the earth, the needy from among mankind" (Prov. 30:14).

David was a man of war, skilled with weaponry of every kind. None was his equal in hand-to-hand combat. Yet the weapons of slander, backbiting, gossip, betrayal and defamation of character seldom make a frontal assault. Our best defense cannot predict their deployment nor ward off their sharpened edges.

There are times we must, with David, admit that our enemies appear as *hunters who track us*:

> [6] *They set a net for my steps;*
>   *my soul was bowed down.*
> *They dug a pit in my way,*
>   *but they have fallen into it themselves. Selah*

The first image (v. 4a) pictures our enemies moving with power, the second (v. 4b) with words; but here they move with stealth. They want to catch us unaware, snatching us mid-stride from our God-appointed course. Yet repeatedly, as here, the Psalms describe the foolhardy nature of such tactics. The trap fails, backfiring upon the hunter and catching him in his own trap.[6] Solomon learned this truth well from his father: "Whoever digs a pit will fall into it, and a stone will come back on him who starts it rolling" (Prov. 26:27). There is indeed a self-defeating nature to slander; yet before we are able to rest in that assurance, we must admit the apparent power of those who slander us.

Few of us find it easy to pray through honestly about how our enemies appear to us. Part of it is the vulnerability of admitting our weakness and fear. The greater struggle, however, is in allowing ourselves to designate them as "enemies." We just don't feel comfortable with the terminology nor its implications. We read the Biblical record and easily enough assign the title to the appropriate characters, but to affix it to someone in our lives is more unset-tling. It seems, well, almost un-Christian to admit to hav-ing enemies. It feels like a failure to have relationships that have descended to such a level.

Jesus, however, never sought to deny the reality of en-emies, only to regulate how we respond to them. Perhaps we are afraid that, if we admit how we feel about such people, we will be unable to restrain the unfettered feel-ings. Such feelings, however, do not dissipate in the dark-ness of a covered heart. Their power only grows, infecting our relationships with a tense distance and our hearts with growing bitterness. In prayer before our Father, we must process through the reality of our feelings and percep-tions—both accurate and inaccurate—honestly assessing our impressions.

An enemy, in the context of David's prayer, might be anyone who or anything which threatens to keep you from your divinely-given purpose. Too often we affix the label to anyone who gets in the way of our plans. This is little more than self-will asserting itself. In prayer we are able to work through our self-centeredness to the place where we can discern between those who upset our plans and those who stand in the way of God's purpose. This also requires praying through to a clear understanding of God's stand-ing in the present circumstances.

My God

As David prayed through to the place where vengeance's grip began to slacken, he turned his eyes from his enemies to his God. He saw God to be *a refuge to enter into*: "Be mer-

ciful to me, O God, be merciful to me, for in you my soul
takes refuge" (v. 1). The verb translated "takes refuge" was
also used to depict retreating soldiers fleeing into the mountains to find a safe place above the danger.[7] The term also
became familiar in phrases like "a rock of refuge," describing a high place to which one could flee from danger
and from whose vantage point one could look down upon
the trouble. Here David's refuge is clearly the mountain
cave into which he and his men had fled. Here he escaped
the vulnerability of the open ranges. Here he was concealed and contained.

The rock of refuge for David was physical, yet it was
more. The stone walls surrounding him were a metaphorical reminder of the divine Rock who was his keeper. Perhaps David called to mind the
great blessing of Moses as he
penned this prayer. "There is
none like God, O Jeshurun,
who rides through the heavens to your help, through the
skies in his majesty [God is
above us]. The eternal God is your dwelling place [God is
around us], and underneath are the everlasting arms [God
is under us]. And he thrust out the enemy before you [God
goes before us]" (Deut. 33:26-27).

*Vengeance begins to lose its grip
on our hearts when God begins
to loom large in our lives.*

Vengeance loses its grip on our hearts when God looms
large in our lives. Praying through to that place takes patience and persistence. As God becomes our focus we, like
David, also begin to see Him as *a shelter to hide under*: ". . .
in the shadow of your wings I take refuge, till the storms
of destruction pass by" (v. 1). The same word for "refuge"

is used here, yet this time the imagery, instead of a cave to enter into, is of a mother eagle gathering her young under her wings.

Again the words of Moses echo through David's prayer. To timid Israelites gathered at Mount Sinai he spoke for God, "You yourselves have seen what I did to the Egyptians, and how I bore you on eagles' wings and brought you to myself" (Exod. 19:4). Forty years later to a new generation of Israelites, he likened God to "an eagle that stirs up its nest, that flutters over its young, spreading its wings, catching them, bearing them on its pinions" (Deut. 32:11).

This is imagery which often comforted David as he purposefully recounted the nature of God in prayer.[8] We too will do well to immerse ourselves in this theme. But what does that mean practically? We come under God's protective wings when in prayer we purposefully recount with faith who He is, what He can do and the promises to which He has committed Himself. This requires confident, resolute praying. It shakes off the feelings of defeat and begins to declare in praise and adoration just who it is our enemies are dealing with—not us, but the God under whose protection we have come by grace.

Vengeance also recedes as we pray through to seeing God as *a deliverer to look up to.*

> [3] *He will send from heaven and save me;*
> *he will put to shame him who tramples on me.*
> *Selah*
> *God will send out his steadfast love and his faithfulness!*

David's problem? It was "him who tramples on me." The answer in such cases is to not only look back but to look up!

The point is that vengeance grows in a closed system. When the problem and all its pieces exist in a closed system where your only hope is you, the only option open to you is taking matters into your own hands. Praying through means broadening your perspective to see that you do not exist in a closed system—God is on high, watching over you. We have not prayed through until we confidently and clearly understand again the greatness and glory of our God. This is what happened as David next prayed, "I cry out to God Most High [notice the vantage point God enjoys over David and all his troubles], to God who fulfills his purpose for me" (v. 2).

This is the key to breaking free of the power of vengeance: "his purpose for me." But honestly, does this really work? Let's ask David. Apparently, this was a repeated refrain of David's life. He again prayed in Psalm 138, "The LORD will fulfill his purpose for me" (v. 8). David had prayed through to the place where his greatest desire was the fulfillment of the purpose of God in and through his life. The pathway to such singular focus requires the bloody death of many lesser desires on the altar of prayer. Such praying involves much travail of soul. Through the passages of life David was able to cling to this singular focus. With all of his failures, the verdict of history vindicated David. Luke, the New Testament historian, records in simple words the epitaph David prayed a lifetime to receive: "David, after he had served the purpose of God in his own generation, fell asleep" (Acts 13:36).

My Responsibilities

Praying through to such singularity of purpose means taking up again the responsibilities which God lays upon me. David closes his prayer by taking up these responsibilities before God. These responsibilities include calming our hearts:

> *7 My heart is steadfast, O God,*
>   *my heart is steadfast!*
> *I will sing and make melody!*
> *8 Awake, my glory!*
>   *Awake, O harp and lyre!*
>   *I will awake the dawn!*

The twice repeated "steadfast" brings before us a word that describes bringing something into being in such a way that its existence is a certainty.[9] It is the word used to describe God establishing the heavens (Prov. 3:19) and the earth (Jer. 33:2). In such praying we are obviously not setting our hearts upon the shifting sands of our own emotions but upon a solid Rock from which they cannot be moved.

This Rock is a God whose purpose is big, encompassing all peoples:

> *9 I will give thanks to you, O Lord, among the peoples;*
>   *I will sing praises to you among the nations.*

This Rock is a God whose love is grand and whose faithfulness is everlasting:

> *10 For your steadfast love is great to the heavens,*
>   *your faithfulness to the clouds.*

Have you honestly prayed through to the place where your heart is calm and resting upon the bedrock of God's purposes and character? Keep praying!

Such calm requires calling on God. Do you, like David, "cry out to God Most High" (v. 2)? I'm confident that if you've read this far you are a person of prayer. Ask yourself, however, who is the God I call to? What do the nature of my utterances in prayer tell me about the nature of the God I pray to? Do you address God as He is, or as you have sketched Him out to be under the pressure of your problems? Low praying betrays a low view of God. A low view of God is nothing other than idolatry. You may address Him with Biblical

Low praying betrays a low view of God. It is your responsiblity to pray to God in a manner befitting who He is.

names and titles, but do your expectations betray a weak view of God? It is your responsibility to pray to God in a manner befitting who He is.

Such praying requires centering on God's glory. In the middle and end of his prayer, David cried out with this refrain: "Be exalted, O God, above the heavens! Let your glory be over all the earth!" (vv. 5, 11). Whenever a writer of Scripture repeats himself, we ought to take notice. Do you see it? This is it, the key. This is the purpose of God for your life and mine. Everything about everything is about the glory of God! If the glory of God is our purpose, we will win. Our circumstances may never change, but we can always glorify God. If we have prayed through to the place where God's glory is our greatest goal, our prayer cannot help but be answered. If God's glory is my goal, taking a pass on vengeance does not guarantee defeat but victory. Only then do the New Testament exhortations regarding vengeance become more than a mocking impossibility.

> If possible, so far as it depends on you, live peaceably with all. Beloved, never avenge yourselves, but leave it to the wrath of God, for it is written, "Vengeance is mine, I will repay, says the Lord." To the contrary, "if your enemy is hungry, feed him; if he is thirsty, give him something to drink; for by so doing you will heap burning coals on his head." Do not be overcome by evil, but overcome evil with good. (Romans 12:18–21)

You can arrive at just such a place of grace and peace, even if those who have wronged you never acknowledge their sin or change their ways. George Herbert was right: "Living well is the best revenge." We aren't done praying until vengeance has released its lock on our lives and grace has our hearts, minds, motives, words and actions firmly in hand.

Praying Through

Before leaving this study take the time to begin praying through the desire for vengeance that may be clawing at your heart.

- Call out to God and honestly tell Him what you think of those who have wronged you. Tell Him how you view what they have done, what they have robbed you of, how they have hurt you. Use whatever metaphors will picture the power of your emotions regarding them.

- Consciously and deliberately turn your heart to God. Take words with you and use them to describe to God how He is your high refuge, lifting you above the fray of troubled relationships. Verbalize to God how you are coming under His protection and how you are looking up to Him in hope. Continue to explore other Biblical metaphors for God's keeping and protection and care.

- In prayer, calm your heart by taking it off of the shifting sands of emotion and establishing it on the solid bedrock of God's character. Anchor your observations to specific statements of Scripture regarding God's nature. Ask God to reveal to you what the nature of your prayers reveal about who you really think He is. Take notes. Confess your low view of God. Receive His forgiveness. Practice making your praying match your theology of God.

- Close by praying through until you recognize God's glory as your greatest goal. Linger here. Don't rush. Leave no pet pursuits untouched. Slay your idols on the altar of God. Pray through till your heart is singularly set upon God's glory alone, even above vindication and punishment of those who have done you wrong.

- Now release to God those who have wronged you. You are not letting them off the hook, you are simply taking them off your hook and placing them on God. Leave to the God of justice to do that which is right.

8

Praying Through Reality

T HE "BIG MO"—David definitely had it. Momentum. It's a sweet word. It's an even sweeter ride. It had been a long time coming, and David had every intention of riding this wave as long as he could.

How do things change so quickly? David momentarily indulged himself with the question as he sat in the tent that had become command central in the wilderness outside of Damascus. *Seems like yesterday I was sleeping in caves, a fugitive from my own people.* He interlaced his fingers and placed them over his head, resting his palms against the back of his head. He leaned back and propped his feet up as a smile began to spread across his face. *Sweet.* It's the only word to describe it. *Sweet.*

David lost himself in a mental litany of his string of recent successes: Saul's death. His anointing as ruler of Judah. Abner's defection to David. Victory over Ish-Bosheth. Anointed by all the tribes as king of Israel. Capture of Jerusalem. Fortification of his capital city. The ark of God brought in. A covenant with God for an everlasting dynasty. Victory over the Philistines. Victory over the Moabites. Victory over Hadadezer of Zobah—extending his control all the way to the Euphrates. And now all-but-certain victory over the Arameans. *A few well-fortified garri-sons here,* David thought to himself, *and Israel will never have been larger, never have been greater.* His smile stretched just a bit broader.

In case you haven't noticed, there is an *I* in Israel. And David was, for the moment, writing it in big, bold upper-case form. What he was forgetting is that the "Big Mo" can also be a big set up. The "Big Mo" engenders feelings of invincibility and over-confidence. The "Big Mo" can woo a man into overextending. The "Big Mo" can create blind-spots. The "Big Mo" can convince you that momen-tum and reputation alone are a sufficient rear guard. But none of that came to David's mind at the moment—he was still stuck on the first letter in Israel.

A commotion outside broke David's trance. As he pulled his feet down and leaned forward Joab appeared inside the tent flap. "Your majesty," he said, "we have trouble."[1]

•   •   •   •   •

Life is messy. Even at its best, life is filled with frustra-tions, setbacks and apparent defeats. Burnt toast, flat tires, missing buttons and slow traffic are destined to be our fare in this world. You're on your way to the most important interview of your life and you spill coffee on your white shirt. You finish washing the car just as the raindrops start to fall. You carry the last shovel-full of snow from your driveway just as the snowplow passes by, filling it in again with three feet of frozen slush.

Life is like that, isn't it? That is why Psalm 60 was writ-ten. The title tells us that David wrote this "when he strove with Aram-naharaim and with Aram-zobah, and when Joab on his return struck down twelve thousand of Edom in the Valley of Salt." Sounds like a victory. In fact if you study the historical records of 2 Samuel 8 and 1 Chronicles 18 you'll find that they too record one victory after another. They read like a slick, four-color promotional piece for the kingdom of Israel.

By now we've fast-forwarded past the persecutions of Saul. David was now anointed as king over all Israel (2 Sam. 5:1–5). He had conquered Jerusalem and made it his capital (2 Sam. 5:6–16). He had brought the ark of the covenant to his city (2 Sam. 6). God had appeared to David, promising him a perpetual dynasty and that the Messiah would come from his lineage (2 Sam. 7). David was definitely on a roll! Out of this unprecedented success the prayer that is Psalm 60 arose. But something seems amiss as David lifts his voice:

> *Life, even at its best, is filled with struggles. Even in our most victorious moments, we struggle against defeat.*

Psalm 60

To the choirmaster: according to Shushan Eduth. A Miktam of David; for instruction; when he strove with Aram-naharaim and with Aram-zobah, and when Joab on his return struck down twelve thousand of Edom in the Valley of Salt.

¹ O God, you have rejected us, broken our defenses;
you have been angry; oh, restore us.

It doesn't fit, does it? The title and the historical records tell of nothing but victory, but this sounds like utter defeat. Why? Because life, even at its best, is filled with struggles. Even in our most victorious moments, we struggle against defeat.

The defeat the psalm speaks of would have never been known to later generations had David not prayed this prayer. We'd have made the mistake of picturing this stage of David's life as nothing but a long string of victories and the peaceful subservience of Israel's neighbors. We'd have wrongly pictured David's life as one with his feet up, an iced tea in his hand and beautifully clad servant girls fanning him with palm fronds. Are the historical records in error? Are they nothing more than kingdom propaganda? No, they are accurate, but selective. They provide an accurate, though incomplete record of David's early years as king. Having finally reached the summit of a mountain, you look out and are struck most by the other peaks extending before you. It's easy to lose sight of the valleys that lay between. I find a measure of relief in knowing that even David's life as king had some valleys between the mountaintops.

The integration of the historical records of 2 Samuel and 1 Chronicles with the title of the psalm seem to paint this picture: David, along with most of his military, was off fighting in the regions of Syria and Jordan. Perhaps he had overextended himself in an attempt to gain valuable ground to the north and east. Whatever the case, the Edomites to the southeast detected a moment of vulnerability. They attacked Israel, apparently even possessing portions of the promised land and perhaps taking captive some of God's people.

For David the news must have come like a slug in the gut. He'd lived life on the run for so long that he'd become accustomed to hardship. But lately things had changed. It seemed that now all the promises of God were coming to fruition. The momentum of success had wooed him into a strange new vulnerability. Just as he thought he'd finally stepped into the flow of God's blessings, the steel-toed boot of Edom kicked him in the teeth.

Know the feeling? That's why we need to pray through reality. Too often as we bow our heads, we silently pass through a door into a world of make-believe. I've seen it happen more times than I can count. I sit and listen to some troubled soul pour out the trials of life. They may fume, rage and convulse in tears. After listening, I ask them if we can pray. They bow their heads and instantly the bitter venomous tones that fumed through clenched teeth are turned to angel-sweet tones as pious-sounding words flow from a serene face. Nothing has changed, except the angle of their head and the fact that the hands that had just been pounding the arm of their chair are folded in apparent calm. Their marriage is still a mess, their boss a jerk, their kids rebellious, the cancer still in their body— but they've gone to a "happy place," a place that does not exist. Too many people use prayer as an escape. Prayer should not be an escape from reality but our ultimate embrace of reality. We need to pray through what really is, not what we'd like it to be. We've come to believe that some things are just not to be brought up in God's presence. So prayer becomes a fruitless game of make-believe instead of the fruitful processing of life's mess with God.

Such praying may offer some temporary therapeutic benefit, but it provides little lasting change.

In Psalm 60 David is praying honestly through reality. No spin. No nuance. Here he is praying about what is. Reflect on how this helps us do the same.

Victory and Hardship

This prayer reminds us that a victorious life is often filled with hardship. Overcomers still have things that must be overcome. This side of heaven there are few pure triumphs. Even in our shining moments we are often beset by less than ideal circumstances. Even when at our best our motives and attitudes still produce spiritual drag, pulling against our progress toward Christ.

David reminds me that even a victorious life involves some struggling. Listen to the warfare language: "O God, you have rejected us, broken our defenses; you have been angry; oh, restore us" (v. 1). The phrase "broken our defenses" may be painting a picture of an army pulling down the walls of a fortified city or bursting through their lines of defense.[2] Warfare was nothing new to David, but surprisingly the struggle here appears to be against the Lord: "O God, *you* have rejected . . . broken our defenses; *you* have been angry." The verbs fire at us in rapid succession. David is desperate, overcome and distraught. Why would God be doing this? It's as though David prayed, "God, I thought you were was supposed to be the defense of my life! While I was keeping my eye on the enemy, you tiptoed off and joined their ranks!" Ever felt that? "Lord, this battle was hard enough when I thought You were on my side! I can't fight all these foes *and* You!" There is no moment quite as desperate as when it *seems* God has abandoned you or joined the other side.

What's going on here? It's possible that sin had entered David's camp, and this raid by Edom was God's discipline. In the days of Joshua, the sin of one man was the reason for Israel's defeat at Ai and the death of thirty-six men. I think, however, there is another possibility that is even more likely. While still camped at Sinai, God told the Israelites,

"I will not drive them out from before you in one year, lest the land become desolate and the wild beasts multiply against you. Little by little I will drive them out from before you, until you have increased and possess the land" (Exod. 23:29–30).

The principle still held true forty years later:

The LORD your God will clear away these nations before you little by little. You may not make an end of them at once, lest the wild beasts grow too numerous for you. But the LORD your God will give them over to you and throw them into confusion, until they are destroyed. (Deut. 7:22–23)

We know that God sets the boundaries of the nations (Gen. 15:18–21). Joshua led the people to basically take possession of the Promised Land in the first seven years after their entrance. After Joshua's death there was still much land to possess, but it amounted to mopping up exercises. Yet the people were not diligent to finish the work. Even in David's day there was much land that had not yet been taken. Through David and then Solomon the borders of Israel finally reached to their God-designed end (2 Sam. 8:1–14; 1 Kings 4:20–25). I believe this tells us the problem was not that God had found sin and that they'd become the object of His discipline but actually that they were in His favor. The struggle David was lamenting was a signal that God was restarting the process that would lead up to the full possession of the land. The struggle was a sign of God's favor, not His disfavor. The struggle was a signal that David was on the right track, not that he had missed God's will.

The struggles we face can be a sign of God's favor, not His disfavor. God accomplishes as much in our warfare as in our winning.

God accomplishes as much in our warfare as in our winning. It's hard to believe, but it's true. All this struggle is preparatory. None of this is the final battle. The battles make us better. They are part of God's plan. Isaac Watts was correct: "I must fight if I would reign." Till you're able to rest in this knowledge, you're not done praying through the hard realities of hardship.

David's prayer also reminds us that even a victorious life involves some shaking. He cried,

> ² *You have made the land to quake; you have torn it open; repair its breaches, for it totters.*

The military metaphor has given way to that of an earthquake. The foundations had been shaken. The nation was not whole, for part of it had been taken captive in Edom. The breech in the border was likened to a fault line in the earth. God had shaken the kingdom. None of this was in the plan—David's plan at least. David had been trying to solidify his reign and had enjoyed unparalleled success, until this. This tasted too much like what he'd had a staple diet of for far too long—defeat.

Why does God do that? Why does He shake the chess-board just when our players are on the verge of victory? It serves as a reminder that as good as it can get here, this is not the end. Don't settle in. Don't settle down. Don't get too satisfied, even with the blessings of God. As pleasant as His grace may be at the moment, it's not about the moment, its about the promise. When we become too comfortable in God-given success, He will shake things up to remind us that the success only comes on the path to a larger purpose.

> At that time his voice shook the earth, but now he has promised, "Yet once more I will shake not only the earth but also the heavens." This phrase, "Yet once more," indicates the removal of things that are shaken—that is, things that have been made—in order that the things that cannot be shaken may remain. (Heb. 12:26–27)

Not even the created order is safe when it comes to God's relentless commitment to fulfill His will! Let us, however, remember: God only shakes us so He can grant us the unshakeable. "Therefore let us be grateful for receiving a kingdom that cannot be shaken, and thus let us offer to God acceptable worship, with reverence and awe, for our God is a consuming fire" (Heb. 12:28–29). Gratitude grows from our confusion when we realize that God shakes our little kingdom so that He might more fully grant us His own unshakeable kingdom. Praying through reality means not saying "Amen" until we have lifted our eyes past the pain of our struggle and thanked God for the better inheritance He's granting us in the process.

As David prays on we learn that even a victorious life involves some staggering.

> *³ You have made your people see hard things;*
>   *you have given us wine to drink that made us stagger.*

The metaphor is now that of a drunkard. It appears God has done the unthinkable—He's baited Israel into drinking themselves silly! Of course God had not intentionally confused David and his court. Nor does He do so in our case. But God does consistently refuse to be confined to our neat little categories. God saw that David's box was too small; his dreams too tiny. His problem was not that he expected too much of God and He'd let him down. His mistake was in expecting too little of God. As a result God was scrambling his categories in order to raise his expectations.

When what we've embraced as reliable markers for reality begin to tumble, we panic. The purpose is to return us to the only fixed point in reality —the Lord.

Isn't this what happened with Job? Job's friends saw life with God as a mathematical equation—obey and be blessed; sin and be disciplined. They left no room for God's inscrutable purposes. In the end God neither performed to their expectations nor explained Himself. He shut their mouths with a series of seventy questions[3] that staggered and silenced Job but returned him to the status of a worshiper (Job 38–42).

We stagger when the fixed points we've been depending upon for equilibrium suddenly begin moving. When what we've embraced as reliable markers for reality begin to tumble, we panic. The purpose is to return us to the only fixed point in reality—the Lord who does not change. When everything begins swinging, swimming and shifting, it is God's invitation to know Him better and worship Him more deeply.

The struggling, shaking and staggering that interrupts our brightest moments are offered to us not necessarily as discipline, but perhaps as a signal of God's favor, of His offer of something lasting and as an invitation to worship.

Victory and Hope

True enough, a victorious life is always filled with hardship, but it is also always filled with hope. As David prays on we discover that praying through reality requires knowing what banner to run to.

> *4 You have set up a banner for those who fear you,*
> *   that they may flee to it from the bow. Selah*
> *5 That your beloved ones may be delivered,*
> *   give salvation by your right hand and answer us!*

In the ancient Near East a banner would at times be raised in preparation for battle. It became a rallying point for warriors organizing themselves for battle. Yet that seems not to be David's point here. The banner here is not a rallying point from which to go engage the enemy but a safe-place to which we may retreat from battle. This is the ensign lifted high so that frightened, confused and doubting soldiers can flee to safer ground. It's the M.A.S.H. unit for wounded soldiers. The banner must be lifted high, because we need to know not only how to advance but when and how to retreat . . . and thus prepare to engage the battle at another time.

The text at this point prescribes a "Selah." This oft repeated word probably signals a rest point in the music. It is a signal for a pause to ponder what has just been said. It's almost a command to "Stop and think this over before you move on." So let's do just that. What is this "banner"? It is that which we run to when we need truth. When confused by the struggling, shaking and staggering, we ask, "What's going on here? What is God doing? How could this happen?"

Ultimately this banner is none other than the Lord Himself (Exod. 17:15). God's Word, His character revealed there, the promises broadcast there, the warnings issued there, the purposes outlined there—flee for safety to the firm, sure Word of God. Praying through means doing exactly what by now you can tell this book is all about: Opening your Bible and pressing through in prayer till its words are your own words arising from your heart. That's why David prayed on to show us that praying through reality requires knowing what word to believe:

> [6] *God has spoken in his holiness:*
> > *"With exultation I will divide up Shechem*
> > *and portion out the Vale of Succoth.*
> [7] *Gilead is mine; Manasseh is mine;*
> > *Ephraim is my helmet;*
> > *Judah is my scepter.*
> [8] *Moab is my washbasin;*
> > *upon Edom I cast my shoe;*
> > *over Philistia I shout in triumph."*

See it? "God has spoken in his holiness." Go back to what God says. David does just that as he draws in and then exhales his next breath—gathering up the promises of God made throughout the history of the nations, but particularly those made to Abraham (Gen. 15). Watch how he does so. He mentions six locations within Israel. Shechem and the Vale of Succoth, located on either side of the Jordan, were the first parts of the land occupied by Jacob. Gilead was Israelite territory east of the Jordan. Manasseh straddled the Jordan. Ephraim was likened to her main defense, or helmet. Judah is called "my scepter." Don't miss that. This was the place from which God's kingdom would extend, where David ruled and from which God's ultimate King, the Messiah, would rule over all. Don't lose sight of the fact that God had just promised David a perpetual dynasty and that the Messiah would come from his line (2 Sam. 7). For David praying through meant going back to the promises of God and holding them before Him again.

David, however, also turned his attention to the nations around Israel. Moab is pictured as a washbasin. The lowest slave washed the feet of the men when they came into the home. Moab would be fit for nothing but as the place for cast off bath water. Edom, the invaders of Israel at this time, was a place upon which David would cast his shoe. Having washed his feet and dumped the remains on Moab, Edom was barely fit as a place to throw his dirty shoes. And Philistia, the perpetual thorn in Israel's side—a shout of triumph will be raised over her!

What is all of this about? It is the sound of a man whose present reality has been shaken, so he is verbally reaching back into the only fixed thing on the horizon—the Word of God—and praying it back to God.

> Since I must fight if I would reign,
> Increase my courage, Lord;
> I'll bear the toil, endure the pain,
> Supported by Thy Word.
> —Isaac Watts

Praying through to hope means knowing what banner to run to, which means knowing what word to believe, which in turn results in knowing what hope to cling to. David prayed,

> *9 Who will bring me to the fortified city?*
> *Who will lead me to Edom?*

The "fortified city" of Edom was none other than Petra, the renown fortress carved from solid stone. Its only entrance is a narrow gorge of almost two miles rising hundreds of feet on either side and barely passable by two horsemen side by side at some places. It was in David's day a mountain stronghold considered completely inaccessible and impregnable. It was humanly impossible to enter Petra, overcome its army, and retrieve what was stolen.

Doesn't sound like much hope. But listen as David prays through and emerges from despair:

> *10 Have you not rejected us, O God?*
> *You do not go forth, O God, with our armies.*
> *11 Oh, grant us help against the foe,*
> *for vain is the salvation of man!*

> [12] *With God we shall do valiantly;*
> *it is he who will tread down our foes.*

Here is the hope into which praying through delivers you: God is for me. I am for God. He has committed Himself to me in amazing promises, and though I don't understand why, I know that He cannot do anything but keep them. Even a victorious life is *sometimes* filled with hardship, but a victorious life is *always* filled with hope. Laying hold of the hope is a matter of knowing what banner to run to, what word to believe and what hope to cling to.

God is for me. I am for God. He has committed Himself to me in amazing promises, and though I don't understand why, I know that He cannot do anything but keep them.

You aren't done praying through until you are firmly standing under the banner of God's truth, your heart has welled up again in fresh trust in His promises and hope has begun to break through again. This is the steadfast reality into which you need to emerge as you pray through the hardships that press upon you even now.

Praying Through

Take some time with God now before you turn away to other pursuits. Pray through the reality of where you find yourself at this moment in time.

- Begin by honestly recounting to God the struggles you are facing. Tell Him where life is a battle. Nothing is too petty if it perplexes you. Be thorough.

- Authentically express to God the dismay you feel over the uncertainty of what you thought was reliable but now is failing you. Tell Him your disappointment of trusted friends letting you down, or of a lost job or whatever has rocked your world lately. Recount the fear this creates.

- Tell God how unsteady you feel. Describe your confusion to Him. Tell Him what you thought you knew but now why that appears not so certain. Ask God to show you His character and purposes afresh.

- Now transition in prayer, purposely and with discipline running to hide under the banner of God's character and promises. Open your Bible. Locate promises that speak to your circumstances. Meditate on them. Turn them back to God in prayer. Decisively plant yourself upon these promises and the character of the God who stands behind them. Plant a flag here and commemorate that today you're taking these promises up afresh in a personal way.

- Now, no matter how impossible your circumstances feel, pray, "With God [I] will do valiantly; it is he who will tread down [my] foes" (v. 12). Claim the necessary victory by faith. Refuse to leave God's presence without hope. Ask God, as the God of hope, to "fill you with all joy and peace in believing, so that by the power of the Holy Spirit you may abound in hope" (Rom. 15:13). As He does, rise and do the next thing you know from God's Word is the right step of obedience.

9

Praying Through Guilt

"YOU!"

The declaration thundered over the lips, down the extended arm and out the boney, pointing finger of the prophet.

King David was not accustomed to the receiving end of prophetic denunciations. Courtiers gasped. The cupbearer nearly choked. Counselors took a step back, as if to avoid the lighting strike of judgment that would surely follow. But what, in any other court and on almost any other day, would have cost the prophet his life was met on this day with an extended silence from the king. It was the longest few moments of David's life. The events of the last twelve months played out in his mind in slow motion, though only a few seconds slipped by imperceptibly.

It had started innocently. The battles had been won, resistance put down, enemies subdued. It is at once both the goal and undoing of every military man. Victory is the objective to be gained at all costs. Yet when it is had, what does he have? Boredom. Uselessness. The soldier longs, not for bloodshed, but for a battle, a purpose, a cause to defend, a principle to advance, something worth living and dying for. But it was the boredom that had done David in. In the vulnerability of idle security, when most other kings had battle lines to visit, David sat out the sultry evenings of late spring in his palace. The oppressive, muggy air hung heavy in his bedroom. Sleep eluded him. He rose to seek a breath of cool air on the roof. He surveyed the scene he'd beheld hundreds of times—his city, the city of God, the city of peace. As David lazily scanned the housetops and darkened, winding streets, his eyes lighted upon something new, something extraordinary.

A woman. Bathing. Naked.

His heart sent his eyes immediately heavenward in holy avoidance. His passions pulled his pupils earthward. As he set his gaze upon her, one could almost hear the clank of chains and slap of manacles—his heart was captive. Without breaking his lustful trance, he summoned his chamber attendant. "Who is she?" he numbly mumbled. The confused attendant hesitantly asked, "Who is who, your majesty?" "There!" his voice intensified as he gestured in annoyance. "One moment, sire," he begged off. Soon he returned, "Sir, her name is Bathsheba." "Get her," was the king's only response as he remained motionless, transfixed upon her beauty.

The pleasures of the night passed quickly. Soon the light of day broke through the balcony that had drawn him into darkness just hours before. David jolted awake and sprang upright in his bed. He looked about him. She was gone. The day seemed dim, there was a weight upon his heart.

She came to his conscious thought but seldom again. Then came a sealed note. The courier had waited dutifully for further orders as the king stared in stunned disbelief at the simple lines. Finally his arms dropped limp at his sides and the small scroll fluttered to the floor. The fleeting glance the courier dared cast enabled him to discern only a few letters: "preg____." He quickly snapped back to attention and dutifully carried out the orders that followed.

There had been a sudden flurry of military correspondence to the front lines. Notes to Joab. Replies in return. Conferences and dinners with an obscure serviceman. Eventually news of a casualty from the battle front. Then a hasty, unceremonious and unpublicized wedding in a backroom of the palace.

Tidy. Swept. Clean. The matter had been dealt with. The king moved on. So did the rumors, but they never reached the king's ears. Soon enough the king held his new son in his arms. He rejoiced, as much as he could through the grey hue that had settled over his heart.

Abruptly David snapped back to a conscious awareness of his surroundings. He glanced around and met the curious expressions and gaping mouths that filled his court. He looked again at Nathan the prophet. Again he repeated, "You are the man!"

David knew he was right.[1]

* * * * *

What is the difference between repentance and remorse? The question demands an answer. Not all that weeps is truly broken. Not every promise of reform produces real change. The Scriptures make clear that "godly grief produces a repentance that leads to salvation without regret, whereas worldly grief produces death" (2 Cor. 7:10). Not all that appears religious in its regret is genuine repentance. It may be nothing more than remorse. Human nature being what it is, an accurate answer to our question is difficult to come by. Psalm 51 is, however, a prayer of true repentance, not mere remorse. This cry arose from the aftermath of David's adulterous rendezvous with Bathsheba. It began in laziness, lust and lies. It issued in a murder, an infant's death and wholesale deception. For the better part of a year, David lived without resolution to his departure from God. The facade stayed in place, but the soul had gone out of his life with God. Then a daring prophet of God appeared in the court and called David on his sin. To his credit, David owned up to his failure. This model of repentant prayer is the result. Nothing is more needed than praying through to full repentance. Remember, however, not all that prays is truly repentant. How do I pray through mere remorse and on to true repentance?

The Depth of My Sin

Praying through to repentance begins with an understanding of the depth of the sin committed. No pretense. No leveraging with God. No efforts to justify self. Repentance begins with an unabashed ownership of the sin.

Psalm 51

To the choirmaster. A Psalm of David, when Nathan the prophet went to him, after he had gone in to Bathsheba.

¹ Have mercy on me, O God,
*   according to your steadfast love;*

> *according to your abundant mercy*
> *blot out my transgressions.*
> ² *Wash me thoroughly from my iniquity,*
> *and cleanse me from my sin!*

Genuine repentance understands *the horror of the sin.* Three words in David's first utterances reveal the recognition of his sin. The word "transgressions" (vv. 1, 3, 13) points to revolt against God. Until we recognize our actions as rebellion against God, we have not prayed through to repentance. The word "iniquity" (vv. 1, 5, 9) describes a twisting of God's ideal and original design. This describes not so much a violent revolt as it does a subtle, sick twisting of God's intention. It is picturesque of what took place on that warm spring night when David caught sight of Bathseba. The divine pattern for marriage was twisted to fit the king's pleasure-driven passion. Then the word "sin" (vv. 2–5, 9) describes missing the mark of God's holiness.

> *Repentant prayer names actions as sin and takes personal responsiblity for them. Repentance puts an ax to all excuse-making.*

Seven times in just the opening four verses David names his actions as sin. Fifteen times in just the first six verses he uses the personal pronouns "I," "me," or "my"—demonstrating the personal responsibility he is taking. Repentance puts an ax to all excuse-making.

David did not stop with confession, but went on to ask for forgiveness. He saw the horror of his sin before God. He asked God to "blot out" his sin (v. 1). The same word was used of the effect of the flood upon every living creature in Noah's day (Gen. 7:23). David was begging God to expunge his sin from his record. In the ancient world writing was done on leather scrolls. Erasures were difficult to make. It involved sponging the ink off the scroll with water, until every trace was gone. David begged God to deluge his sins in the flood of His forgiveness.

David also asked God to "wash" him of his iniquity (v. 2). This word described the cleaning of clothes that had been contaminated—perhaps by leprosy or illness. Don't picture a modern washing machine set to the gentle cycle for delicate fabrics. Rather the image is of a woman hunched along a river bank, beating the filth from the cloth with a rock. Genuine repentance understands that the removal of sin's filth is an unpleasant business.

Then David asked God to "cleanse" him from his sin (v. 2). He chose a word that speaks of ritual or ceremonial cleansing. David saw his sin as shutting him out from God, and he longed to be restored to the intimacy of worship. Real repentance is horrified over its sin. It knows that no wink of God's eye will suffice, but that there must be a deep purging of the inmost being for restoration to God.

Remorse is worried about self, repentance is concerned for the image of God. For this reason repentant praying identifies *the focal point of the sin*:

> *³ For I know my transgressions,*
> *and my sin is ever before me.*
> *⁴ Against you, you only, have I sinned*
> *and done what is evil in your sight,*
> *so that you may be justified in your words*
> *and blameless in your judgment.*

How could David say that his sin was against God only? What about Bathsheba? Uriah her husband? The baby that died as a result? What about his family? Her family? The nation?

Certainly David sinned against all of them, and to the degree it was possible, he needed to confess his sin against them and beg their forgiveness. While that is appropriate and necessary, genuine repentance is most horrified over sin because of a fresh view of God in His holiness. My sin is first and foremost an assault on God. God is the moral standard of the universe. If there were no God there would be no morality—no one to gauge right and wrong by. The result would be that there would be nothing to define sin against our families, churches or community. So, with a new understanding of holiness, real repentance sees clearly the focal point of sin—God Himself. This, perhaps more than anything else, ushers in a new understanding of the depth of my sin.

In this new light repentant prayers describe *the essence of the sin*. Was this a blunder? A mistake? An error in judgment? Is temptation to blame? An evil environment? Or maybe the devil? Repentance points no fingers.

> *5 Behold, I was brought forth in iniquity,*
> *   and in sin did my mother conceive me.*
> *6 Behold, you delight in truth in the inward being,*
> *   and you teach me wisdom in the secret heart.*

Repentance understands there is a fundamental and powerful threat to our hopes. This enemy is all the more powerful because it does not come from without, but from within. I have to face the fact that my greatest menace is me. I am my own worst enemy. David Larsen put it well: "At the center of 'sin' is that proud, perpendicular pronoun "I"! There it is, unbent and unbowed, the assertion of self in rebellion and revolt against a holy God."[2]

The London Times once ran an article inviting responses to the question "What is Wrong with the World?" Answers flooded in, casting blame in every direction. The submission by G.K. Chesterton, however, seemed to end the discussion. His reply read simply:

> In regards to your question: "What is wrong with the world?"
> I am.
>
> Yours truly,
> G.K. Chesterton.

Repentance recognizes and gives expression to the depth of our sin. True, but it also moves us beyond confession. There is no where else to begin, but there is somewhere else to go. Repentance also understands the depth of my need.

The Depth of My Need

Remorse and repentance fundamentally differ over the place "I" and "God" are to be given. Repentance, it is true, receives an entirely new understanding of the depth of my need. It even gives expression to these needs, but it begins hesitantly. Repentance knows it has nowhere to stand but upon grace. David's expression of need began as wishes, not rights. While the English forms in verses seven and eight appear as commands, in Hebrew the verbal form represents more of a wish. He was not demanding his rights, but audibly longing for God's mercy.[3] Thus he prays,

> [7] *Purge me with hyssop, and I shall be clean;*
> *   wash me, and I shall be whiter than snow.*
> [8] *Let me hear joy and gladness;*
> *   let the bones that you have broken rejoice.*

These are the deep longings of David's repentant heart. These are not rights, but longings only to be gazed upon from afar, unless grace breaks through.

God does not owe us anything; repentance understands that. Yet as we exhale our confession of sin, we inhale faith. Thus David moves from his wishes (vv. 7–8) to specific, faith-filled, grace-dependant imperatives:

> [9] *Hide your face from my sins,*
> *   and blot out all my iniquities.*
> [10] *Create in me a clean heart, O God,*
> *   and renew a right spirit within me.*
>
> [11] *Cast me not away from your presence,*
> *   and take not your Holy Spirit from me.*
> [12] *Restore to me the joy of your salvation,*
> *   and uphold me with a willing spirit.*

Real repentance realizes that the time for self-reformation is long past. We must see that our impotency can never bring order to the quagmire we have created through sin. We must come to that painful place where we see ourselves as spiritual quadriplegics plunged in the sea of our own sinful consequences. All our best devices for self-rescue are fruitless. We either cast ourselves upon the gracious arms of a loving Savior who has made provision for our sin, or we sink in self-dependance to an eternity of suffering. In the face of its sin, remorse redoubles its efforts at reformation, while repentance rests in grace.

In the face of its sin, mere remorse redoubles its efforts at reformation; true repentance rests in grace.

The Depth of My Responsibility

With repentance comes not only restored fellowship but restored responsibility. When word of God's pardon had sunk in, David realized he was responsible to respond to God's grace. Forgiveness brings accountability. David displays a subtle shift in attitude as he embraces the grace of God and prays through to repentance.

A repentant heart determines, *I will warn others.* David prayed,

> *13 Then I will teach transgressors your ways,*
> *and sinners will return to you.*

No greater sermon about sin is ever preached than by the one who knows himself to be the sinner. Perhaps the recording of this very prayer was the greatest fulfillment to David's responsibility to warn of the follies of sin.

A repentant heart also determines, *I will praise God.*

¹⁴ Deliver me from bloodguiltiness, O God,
O God of my salvation,
and my tongue will sing aloud of your righteousness.
¹⁵ O Lord, open my lips,
and my mouth will declare your praise.

As a former slave trader John Newton knew the deep revelation of his sinfulness before God. He also knew the "Amazing Grace" of God through Jesus Christ that liberated him from that sin. How fitting that his song has become the favorite of redeemed sinners through the centuries. The last line of Newton's famous hymn echoes the repentant one's commitment to praise:

> When we've been there ten thousand years,
> Bright shining as the sun,
> We've no less days to sing God's praise
> Than when we first begun.

A repentant heart also determines, *I will remain broken.* The only thing harder than being broken is staying broken. Somewhere in the wake of joy that follows the flood of God's pardon, there often comes a quiet whisper: "You're doing OK now. You're getting along admirably. You've really pulled yourself together!" Even a moment's hesitation here moves us off the altar of brokenness and fashions our "repentance" into an idol.

¹⁶ For you will not delight in sacrifice, or I would give it;
you will not be pleased with a burnt offering.
¹⁷ The sacrifices of God are a broken spirit;
a broken and contrite heart, O God, you will not despise.

David knew that he was helpless to bring any sacrifice to God for his sin, other than the sacrifice of a broken heart. Don't forget that David had fasted and prayed to get God to change His mind about the death of his infant son (2 Sam. 12:16–17). Did he make frantic promises of reform? Did he offer to sacrifice anything in exchange for his son's life? I probably would have. But we need to learn the lesson that David was learning, the lesson his predecessor to the throne had failed to learn: "To obey is better than sacrifice" (1 Sam. 15:22).

Oswald Chambers has wisely observed, "The counterfeit of obedience is a state of mind in which you work up occasions to sacrifice yourself."[4] Repentance is not a momentary act, but an enduring new orientation to God, myself and my circumstances.

Charles Colson describes it this way: "Repentance is the process by which we see ourselves, day by day, as we really are: sinful, needy, dependant people. It is the process by which we see God as he is: awesome, majestic, and holy."[5]

The Depth of the Repercussions

Even a small pebble sends rings to the far side of the pond. Inevitably the consequences of our sin spill over into the lives of those around us. Witness David's infant son. The shockwaves of his sin continued reverberating through his family for the rest of his life. How could his capital city and the nation as a whole escape the consequences of his actions? David knew that they could not apart from God's mercy, so he prayed,

> ¹⁸ *Do good to Zion in your good pleasure;*
> *build up the walls of Jerusalem;*
> ¹⁹ *then will you delight in right sacrifices,*
> *in burnt offerings and whole burnt offerings;*
> *then bulls will be offered on your altar.*

Let's face it—our sin affects others. We may ask God to minimize the collateral damage, but we cannot demand it. When the result of our sin detonates, it is never a surgical strike. There is hope, however, for not only does our sin affect others, but our prayers do too.

We must pray that God will minimize the damage our sin has caused others. Not only does our sin affect others, but our prayers do too.

British evangelist Gipsy Smith was once asked how to get a revival started. He wisely answered: "Go home, lock yourself in your room, kneel down in the middle of the floor. Draw a chalk mark around yourself and ask God to start the revival inside that chalk mark. When He has answered your prayer, the revival will be on."

Simply stated, he was demanding that we pray through to genuine repentance. We must not stop short of the real thing. The difference between mere remorse and real repentance is the difference between heaven and hell, bliss and torment, praising and cursing, God and Satan. Both may evoke tears, pray prayers, look religious and promise reformed behavior, but they are different.

Remorse is sorrow for being caught; repentance is grief over the sin. Remorse is distress over the consequences;

repentance is brokenness over rebellion against a holy God. Remorse is temporary and fleeting, but repentance is lasting and life-changing. Remorse is the embarrassed cry of an unbroken soul being caught red-handed, while repentance is the believer's cry of horror over the darkness of his own soul. Remorse hides self-will under the cloak of contrition. When the spot light is off, self-will crawls out from under the wraps to ascend the throne once again. Real repentance, on the other hand, comes clean, slays self-will and ushers Christ back to His rightful place on the throne of our lives. Real repentance begins in a moment but becomes an abiding attitude and orientation to life.

Mere remorse is Satan's tool to torment a bankrupt soul, to deceive that soul into believing it has done business with God. Repentance is God's gift to liberate a soul that has been undone before His infinite holiness and to usher it into the new life He offers in Christ.

From the outside, remorse and repentance look much the same. On the inside they are as different as heaven and hell, bliss and torment, praising and cursing, God and Satan. Pray through until you've got the real thing.

Praying Through

Do you need to pray through to repentance? Get alone with God and use Psalm 51 as your guide.

- Take the time to still your heart before God. Then ask Him to search you and to impart an understanding of the depth of your sin. Wrestle through until you see the horrors of your sin, not simply for its consequences but for what it is before God. Ask God to show you His holiness, no matter what it exposes or the pain it causes. Confess that the problem is not simply what you have *done*, but who you *are*. Don't hurry on from here, pray through to ownership of your sin.

- Express to God what you wish Him to do. Admit you have no right to demand and no power to compel His response. Then specifically ask God to cleanse you of your sin, based upon the finished work of Christ's atonement. Thank Him for His forgiveness. Ask God to recreate you from the inside out. Lay out with God specific plans for your cooperation in that transformation (disciplines with Scripture, prayer, fellowship, worship, etc.). This is not flippant; pray through until you know the release of grace in your soul. Search the Scriptures, claim its promises. Name them before God. Record them in a journal. Choose to believe them.

- Breathe deeply of God's grace and praise Him; worship Him and sing of His mercy. Choose to embrace the ministry of being a living example of humility and repentance. Ask God to guard you from the pride of false humility!

- Admit to God that your sin has brought devastating consequences to others around you. Name the consequences you can see or worry about. Pray for those people, asking God to extend His mercy to them and to spare them, as far as possible, from the effects of your sin. List those from whom you must seek forgiveness and to whom you must make restitution.[6] This may prove costly, but here is where repentance separates itself from mere remorse.

10

Praying Through Personal Disaster

THE JAGGED rocks ripped at the tender skin on the souls of his feet. With mincing steps and tear-streaked cheeks, David wailed his way out of Jerusalem, across the Kidron Valley, toward the Mount of Olives and the Jordan beyond. His wives and children dejectedly followed in his mournful train—fear hastening them on, sorrow slowing their steps. With an almost involuntary pause, David came to a halt, turned and looked back at his royal city and the dreams he was leaving behind. The train of family, loyalists, military men and even subservient but faithful foreigners continued their march, filing past their king.

King! Indeed. Did the title still apply?

The approach of one unlikely character drew the king's attention out of his stunned preoccupation. "Ittai," the sovereign said, "Why should you come along with us? Go back and stay with King Absalom. You are a foreigner, an exile from your homeland. You came only yesterday. And today shall I make you wander about with us, when I do not know where I am going? Go back, and take your countrymen."

In a thick, foreign accent, but with unmistakable resolve, the converted Gentile replied, "As surely as the LORD lives, and as my lord the king lives, wherever my lord the king may be, whether it means life or death, there will your servant be."

The corners of David's mouth rose only slightly as a defiant surge of encouragement fought its way temporarily through the gloom of his heart. "Go ahead, march on."

Crowds gathered to watch the sad spectacle. The sound of weeping filled the air as the sorry band retreated from the stronghold of Zion.

As the throng moved toward the Kidron Valley, the priest, Zadok, and a band of Levites hustled down the road to catch the king. They moved with haste but carefully, for they carried the ark of the covenant. Gingerly setting the ark upon the ground the Levites stepped back as Abiathar began offering sacrifice upon sacrifice until the entire refugee remnant had exited the city.

The ark—the symbol and center of God's presence. How could David go on without knowing God's favor? Had he not seen people die for mishandling the ark? Had he not personally witnessed the power and blessing of proximity to God's presence? Had he not celebrated in bringing it to his city? With resignation in his voice he commanded the priest, "Take the ark of God back into the city." As if in reply to their bewilderment, David went on, "If I find favor in the LORD's eyes, He will bring me back and let me see it and His dwelling place again. But if He says, 'I am not pleased with you,' then I am ready; let Him do to me whatever seems good to Him."

The king turned and walked away, leaving behind him Zion, the ark, the kingdom. As he trudged up Olivet the crowds heard the anguished cries his heart could no longer contain. They witnessed the self-imposed shower of dust upon their king's head as he wailed along the road, wincing at every sharp stone beneath his bare feet.

As David crested the summit of the Mount of Olives, he encountered more supporters wishing to display their loyalty. Hushai pledged his loyalty but was commissioned to return and to shuttle reports to the king in exile. A bit further Ziba approached with a string of donkeys and hundreds of food provisions for the fugitive monarch and his followers.

A bit further down the road, it was hard to tell whether David first felt or heard the railing denouncements of one Shimei. Undaunted by the surrounding troops and supporters, this Saul-loyalist pelted the king with angry stones and rained curses upon him. "Get out, get out, you man of blood, you scoundrel!" he screamed in bitter voice. "The LORD has repaid you for all the blood you shed in the household of Saul, in whose place you have reigned. The LORD has handed the kingdom over to your son Absalom. You have come to ruin because you are a man of blood!"

Abishai, the king's protector, reached for his sword, but David's own hand, which had many times similarly reached for the blade while in battle, now came firmly to rest upon his, stopping him short. "If he is cursing because the LORD said to him, 'Curse David,' who can ask, 'Why do you do this?'"

Stunned eyes fell to the ground as the deposed king said, "Leave him alone; let him curse, for the LORD has told him to." The procession turned and plodded on in a silence broken only by the continuing curses of Shimei as he ran alongside screaming, throwing stones and calling down God's wrath upon David and his brood.

Bivouacking some twenty miles through the wilderness brought the band to the banks of the Jordan. The hour was late. Darkness was upon them. Defeat reverberated in their hearts. The fording of the river and a relative measure of safety would have to wait till first light. As the aching muscles of his back settled for the night in the dirt and he pulled up a stone-pillow for his head, David stared off into the night and contemplated the divine promise of a kingdom and a progeny. Just hours before it all seemed so solid, but now it more resembled the vaporous mists of the night that began to blanket them. When that which is most sacred is stolen by one who is most loved, a fog of confusion begins to settle in. When you lose your throne it can make you wonder if God is still on His.[1]

· · · · ·

What do you do when the roof caves in? That is what Augustan Sanou and his neighbors found themselves asking. Augustan, like nearly every other resident of Burkina Faso, relies upon subsistence farming for survival. Inside their homes of red mud brick they pray yearly for generous rains. Life at its best is a struggle in this west African nation. Families, if they are fortunate, are able to harvest just enough to get them through to the next planting season. This year Augustan and his neighbors were rejoicing as the rainy season was offering plentiful showers. Then the roof caved in, literally. The heavier than normal rains soaked their homes and, in the early morning hours the roof of Augustan's neighbor collapsed under the weight— killing their newborn son and seriously injuring the father.

Life is always full of challenges, but what do you do when troubles compound, overwhelm and threaten to crush you? The prescript of Psalm 3 signals that it is a prayer that arose from personal disaster. David's son Absalom wanted to kill him and take his kingdom. Think of it.

Psalm 51 was chronologically the last psalm with a historical footnote. Plenty of time had passed between that psalm and this, but there is a direct and very sad link. David's liaison with another man's wife set in motion a tsunami of consequences that rocked his world for generations to come.[2] Adultery. Pregnancy. Murder. Marriage. Coverup. Exposure. Repentance. Forgiveness. But the prophet had told David, "Now therefore the sword shall never depart from your house, because you have despised me and have taken the wife of Uriah the Hittite to be your wife. Thus says the LORD, 'Behold, I will raise up evil against you out of your own house'" (2 Sam. 12:10–11).

The reverberations of David's sin began to evidence themselves immediately. The child died. Tamar, David's daughter, was later raped by her half-brother Amnon. Frustrated by his father's inaction, Absalom avenged his sister's rape by murdering Amnon. Absalom fled into exile. Eventually he was restored to Israel but remained estranged from David. Absalom plotted, schemed and eventually hatched his plans for a coup of his father's government. Chapters 15–17 of Second Samuel provide the sordid details of intrigue, betrayal, espionage, avarice, rape and suicide.

Having fled his capital city and endured a traumatic twenty-mile flight to the Jordan, David and those with him awaited dawn's first light and hope for a new day. What must that night have been like? Instead of the comforts of the royal palace, David settled himself in the dust, pulled up a rock for a pillow and stared off into the night sky.

Think of the sudden losses David had incurred: the loss of God's favor, an infant son dead, a daughter raped, a son murdered by another son, the kingdom stolen by his own son, betrayed by his friend and counselor Ahithopel, driven from his capital city, removed from the temple and ark, his reputation besmirched, the throne stolen and the kingdom in jeopardy.

Indeed, when that which is most sacred is stolen by one who is most loved, a fog of confusion begins to settle in. When you've lost your throne, it makes you wonder if God is still on His. How are we supposed to pray then? Psalm 3 exists to answer that question.

Personal disaster brings a fog of confusion, and makes you wonder if God is still on His throne. How are we supposed to pray then? Psalm 3 exists to answer that question.

Interestingly Psalm 4 has become known as an evening psalm, while Psalm 3 is known as a morning psalm. Perhaps both were recorded about this time. Did David pen this prayer the morning after the coup, perhaps rising before the others in his escape party, shaking the dust from his tunic and finding a quiet spot to seek God's presence? What we do know is that Psalm 3 shows us how to pray when the roof caves in.

Psalm 3

A Psalm of David, when he fled from Absalom his son.

¹ O LORD, how many are my foes!
Many are rising against me;

² *many are saying of my soul,*
 there is no salvation for him in God.

Selah

Pray Accurately

When personal disaster strikes we must pray accurately about our enemies. Sometimes honesty requires admitting *my enemies are multiplying*: "O LORD, how many are my foes! Many are rising against me; many are saying of my soul, there is no salvation for him in God" (vv. 1–2). The repetitions signal David's outlook: "how many . . . many . . . many. . . ." David was not being melodramatic—his enemies *were* multiplying. In fact the nation as a whole put their backing with Absalom (2 Sam. 15:12–13, 16:7–8, 17:11, 18:7). The many are collectively designated simply as "foes." The word describes those who "cause him distress by crowding him into a narrow place."[3]

Honestly, doesn't life feel like that at times? Not many mornings leave us taking up weapons in a military conflict, but we all awake to a world of competition. The stakes are high: job security, physical security, financial security, family security, spiritual security. The weapons are words, more often than not—power plays, manipulation, half-truths, unethical practices, rumors are the daily ammunition. Life is a battle. We need to pray through it on a war footing. Indeed my prayers must sometimes admit *my enemies are mutinous*.

There are some folks who want your head—more accurately, they want your job, your spouse or your office. David used the verb "rising against" to describe the coup.

It refers to a staged rebellion. David was telling God, "Not only am I outnumbered, but I have been out-maneuvered!" Ever had the one you trust the most turn on you, perhaps finding out too late how long the plot had been brewing? Another king would utter his last words to his betrayer: "*Et tu, Brute?*"

Accurate praying also requires seeing that *my enemies are muttering.* David prayed, "Many are saying of my soul, there is no salvation for him in God" (v. 2). Perhaps he was referring to Shimei, who assailed him as he fled Jerusalem,

> Get out, get out, you man of blood, you worthless man! The LORD has avenged on you all the blood of the house of Saul, in whose place you have reigned, and the LORD has given the kingdom into the hand of your son Absalom. See, your evil is on you, for you are a man of blood. (2 Sam. 16:7–8)

Were Shimei's words false? No, perhaps from a bitter heart but not entirely in error. There were things God withheld from David, such as building the temple, because of the blood he had shed (1 Chron. 22:8). Inaccuracy was not the problem. It was the insinuation that he was beyond God's grace: "Not even God can help you now!" It's one thing for friends to desert you and family members to design against you, but it is altogether a different thing when they try to rob you of God. The power of a rumor is an awesome thing—not only in shaping public perception but also personal outlook. We must pray through to a confident stand in God's grace, even when the roof is caving in over our heads.

This signals that, while we must pray accurately about our enemies, we must also pray believingly about our God.

> *³ But you, O LORD, are a shield about me,*
> *my glory, and the lifter of my head.*

Pray Believingly

David's next breath marked a clear transition in his focus: *"But you,* O LORD" (v. 3). How different is God than are the multiplying, mutinous, muttering rebels! Praying through personal disaster requires getting our eyes squarely and believingly on God.

David looked at God and said, *He is my guard!* "But you, O LORD, are a shield about me." Frequently throughout the Scriptures the imagery of a shield is a metaphor for God's protection of His own. By faith David was declaring that the situation was the ex-

We must be willing to listen to reproof; but when the words are designed to wound and not to heal, we must pray through to the place where the truth is louder than the lies.

act opposite of what his enemies were reporting. They were saying that God had given up on David and was judging him. The truth is that God was standing with him and surrounding him.

It takes great faith to pray through the barrage of public opinion about you and emerge into the truth of who you are in Christ. We must be willing to listen to reproof; but when the words are designed to wound and not to heal, we must pray through to the place where the truth is louder than the lies.

David also said of God, *He is my glory!* "But you, O LORD, are . . . *my glory.*" This could mean either "You are my Glorious One" (referring to the character of God) or "the One who restores my glory" (referring to the actions of God). In view of the circumstances, while the former is unquestionably true, the latter is the more likely meaning here.[4] Think of the glory stripped from David in the past twenty-four hours! This is a prayer of great faith: "O Lord, Your purposes for me are not yet over. I don't have to seek to establish my own glory. My times are in Your hands!"

Are you at peace with that? Too often we believe our glory lies down the path of self-promotion or self-affirmation. Those who walk in faith understand that glory only comes after divine affirmation. Pray through to the place where you can say to God, "Whom have I in heaven but you? And there is nothing on earth that I desire besides you" (Ps. 73:25).

David also said of God, *he is my guarantee*! "But you, O LORD, are . . . the lifter of my head." This is not the last chapter. I will rise again. God will raise me up. I will be back. Can you affirm that in faith before God? You don't have to strike back, pay back or get back—because God's got your back. David knew well the promises God had made to him, and he knew they were guaranteed by the unalterable character of the divine nature. It is an act of supreme faith to pray these promises into concrete reality when the roof is caving in over your head. Don't say the final "Amen" until you've prayed through to that place.

> [4] *I cried aloud to the LORD,*
> *and he answered me from his holy hill. Selah*

Pray Honestly

Faith must lead the way, not feelings, but confident faith does not deny honest feelings. These must be prayed through. Hear David, "I cried aloud to the LORD" (v. 4). The verb form can point to repeated action: "I was crying" or "as often as I cried."[5] How many tears did David shed as he made his way out of Jerusalem, across the wilderness and to the Jordan? We are told that he climbed the Mount of Olives "weeping as he went, barefoot and with his head covered" (2 Sam. 15:30). David was utterly devastated. His mourning knew no restraints. There was no regal posturing, no masks to be worn. He was a broken man. When those with him saw his honest emotion they also "covered their heads, and they went up, weeping as they went."

Kathleen Norris says that the psalms "defeat our tendency to try to be holy without being human first."[6] Praying through personal disaster is not a tidy spiritual exercise. It does not fit a schedule. It does not remain neatly under wraps. It often does not conform to acceptable, public, "Christian" demeanor. Praying through often requires many boxes of tissue. It produces red, puffy eyes and a runny nose. We want so desperately to be holy without being honest. God won't allow it. Praying through won't be turned back by unwieldy emotions.

We keep praying through because on the other side of all the emotion we find, like David, "he answered me from his holy hill" (v. 4). By "holy hill" David means Mount Zion, Jerusalem. It was the place of the temple and God's manifest presence. When Abiathar, Zadock and the Levites came after the fleeing David with the ark of the covenant, he had commanded that they return it to the temple where it belonged (2 Sam. 15:24–26). At the time he said, "If I find favor in the eyes of the LORD, he will bring me back and let me see both it and his dwelling place. But if he says, 'I have no pleasure in you,' behold, here I am, let him do to me as seems good to him" (2 Sam. 15:25–26). Now, somehow, God had come to him in his broken distress, and through his tears David heard God's voice whisper again His favor. Absalom might have set himself up as king in Jerusalem, but it was God who still reigned from there!

How had God "answered" David from Mount Zion? Had he sent a prophet with word of His favor? Had His Spirit simply affirmed to David's heart His promises again? We don't know. In whatever way it happened, God had made it so that even though David honestly had to admit "I'm crying!" he could also say, "I'm confident!" He prayed,

> ⁵ *I lay down and slept;*
> *I woke again, for the LORD sustained me.*

The "I" is emphatic: "*I*, even *I*, *a guy in my situation*! *I* lay down and slept!"

Though hunted relentlessly by his enemies, David could lie down and sleep in peace. Behold, the power of praying through!

As a hunted fugitive without knowledge of the enemy's location, speed of pursuit or number, David lay down in the dust along the banks of the Jordan River and went to sleep. How? And remember that this is the morning psalm, a psalm of testimony about what had happened. The evening psalm, the psalm of faith, reports, "In peace I will both lie down and sleep; for you alone, O LORD, make me dwell in safety" (Ps. 4:8). Again, how?

Insomniacs unite! Behold, the power of praying through! "David was as peaceful and secure on the open plain as he was in his own palace."[7]

As amazing as was his sleep, there was an even greater miracle: "I awoke again, for the LORD sustained me" (v. 5). It had not been David's military prowess, his knowledge of the wilderness or his cunning mind that had kept him. The Lord was his confidence, because He was his keeper.

> *⁶ I will not be afraid of many thousands of people*
> *who have set themselves against me all around.*

The designation "many thousands" was not an exaggeration, for all the tribes of Israel had followed Absalom. Nor were they faceless foes. They had been *his* people! Yet his eyes closed, his body relaxed, his spirit was at rest— because he honestly prayed through from crying to confidence. It is just this sort of honest praying that puts us in a position to pray confidently about our hope.

Pray Confidently

In the rising tide of hope that swelled within him, David closed his prayer with two confident assertions about God. In both cases he turned the phrases of his enemies back upon them by taking them up before God.

David was confident: *The Lord will fight for me!* He prayed,

> [7] *Arise, O* LORD!
> *Save me, O my God!*
> *For you strike all my enemies on the cheek;*
> *you break the teeth of the wicked.*

The command "*Arise*, O LORD!" comes from the same root word he began the prayer with: "Many are *rising up* against me" (v. 1). As he began to pray, David saw nothing but the rising menace of his enemies. As he prayed through David remembered that no enemy arises against God's own, but what He arises on their behalf. Knowing this we may call on God to rise up in response to them.

Actually the expression "Arise, O LORD!" was a common war cry. It was used when the Israelites took the ark of the covenant into battle. Because God manifested His presence above the cover of the ark, it was associated with the presence and power of God. When Israel broke camp in the wilderness, it was because the cloud of God's glory rose up from above the ark and began to move. On such occasions Moses cried out, "Arise, O LORD, and let your enemies be scattered, and let those who hate you flee before you" (Numb. 10:35).

David boldly calls on God to rise up and fight for him; then he prays, "Save me, O my God!" The word for "save" is from the same word David's enemies had used against him: "there is no *salvation* for him in God" (v. 2). David was calling on God to do the very thing his enemies said He would not do. He prayed for God to save him by humiliating ("For you strike all my enemies on the cheek") and disarming ("you break the teeth of the wicked") all his enemies.[8]

David was confident: *The Lord will deliver me!* He prayed,

> *⁸ Salvation belongs to the LORD;*
> *your blessing be on your people! Selah*

David clearly signaled that the pattern and substance of which he has been praying belong not simply to him as the Lord's anointed, but to all God's people. In fact the word "salvation" is the one from which the name *Yeshua* (Jesus) comes.[9] Interestingly the pathway David walked as he departed Jerusalem was the same one Jesus would travel as He made His way to the garden in Gethsemane.[10] There David's Savior and ours, would also be betrayed by a friend. From there the nation, His nation, would turn against Him. Jesus, however, did not flee. He stayed. He prayed through and "for the joy that was set before him he endured the cross, despising its shame" (Heb. 12:2). Jesus died, for David and for us. David looked forward in faith to the deliverance God would bring; we, because of Christ, can look back and count it a done deed. With the eyes of faith we can pray with even more confidence than David did.

Praying Through

Use Psalm 3 as a guide to pray through your own personal disaster:

- Remember, devastation of the magnitude this psalm describes did not begin (though it is often revealed) in a single hour. Neither is it resolved with a passing prayer. Praying *through* requires tenacity and enduring faith.

- Tell God exactly what you perceive about those who are at the fore of this attack. Admit that what you perceive may not be accurate. Ask God to adjust your view.

- Set your eyes upon God in faith. Despite your feelings affirm that God is your shield and guard. In the midst of the shame, take God as your greatest glory and the guard of your reputation. Affirm in faith that He lifts your head that has been downcast in disgrace. Choose to affirm the promises of God for your future (e.g., Jer. 29:11; Phil. 1:6; Rev. 3:21).

- Even as you will your way ahead in faith, be honest about your feelings. Cry, literally, before God. Know that your tears are as audible to God as your words. Don't shortchange yourself or God at this point; it is crucial. On the other hand, don't let yourself be mired in the emotion, but move on to confident prayers of faith.

- Confidently tell the Lord you know He is fighting for you. Know He is rising up to your defense. Thank the Lord for the deliverance from the penalty and power of sin He has provided through Christ. Pray prayers worthy of an overcomer!

- Realize that you may need to pray through these steps again and again. Know that this is the way through to a new day. Don't be dissuaded. Nor are all these steps woodenly sequential. As long as it takes, keep cycling through these elements of overcoming faith and prayer.

11

Praying Through Spiritual Drought

THE YELP of a jackal echoed from somewhere just beyond the crest of a nearby hill. A scorpion scurried for refuge beneath a rock. The sand at his feet bore the unmistakable sidewinding trail of a viper. A vacuous wind as from a blast furnace met David full in the face. Grit pelted his exposed skin. The Judean wilderness can be an unforgiving place, but at the moment forgiveness didn't feel like his greatest need.

It was a mythical land, fit only as a retreat for eccentric prophets and an escape for fugitives. David had been to the desert before, but never for a reason quite like this. He wasn't feeling particularly prophetic at the moment. That left fugitive as his only option. It fit. A fugitive, not from justice, but from his son, his people, his city, his nation.

His legs, wearied by the wasted motion of fleeing through sand, seemed distant and remote, unwilling or unable to hear the commands his mind sent to hurry along the way. But hurry he must, for it was no telling just where the marauding hordes were in their pursuit. Pushing, racing, stumbling, David staggered ahead toward an as-yet-undetermined destination.

"The children must rest!" someone in the party cried

as they had innumerable times in the preceding hours. His small band pleaded for a break.

"Fine. Stop. Rest, if you must."

Leaving them with their scant provisions, David stumbled on, putting definition to the distance he felt from even the loyalists who had fled Jerusalem with him. He was emotionally alone; he might as well be in physical solitude as well.

Circling the hill, David finally gave his legs permission to give out. His body slammed hard to the desert floor as he crumpled in a semi-controlled collapse. The wineskin slung over his shoulder gave up nothing as he held it aloft to his lips. The empty hide was already growing brittle in the searing sun. The opposite walls of David's throat seemed to touch and not release as he attempted a swallow. The king seemed almost to be watching on in disbelief, as if standing outside himself.

How? How does a king come to this? And what about God? What about the hours spent in adoring worship at the tabernacle? What of the presence of God manifested between the cherubim's wings above the mercy seat? Was that vision of God's glory and greatness a mirage?

Fine, take the kingdom! You can have Jerusalem! I don't need the palace. Just give me . . . my God. My God! Why? He would have wept if his body could have mustered the moisture. But dry sobs sometimes have to do for a soul seemingly abandoned by its God.[1]

· · · · ·

The Mojave Dessert's late summer sun blistered the body of Lance Corporal Jason Rother as he fought for his life. Having been assigned to night desert maneuvers on August 31, Rother was to have been picked up by one o'clock the next afternoon. However, what proved to be a tragic communications miscue left Corporal Rother under the scorching sun that can surge past 110 degrees. Almost two full days passed before a search team began seeking the whereabouts of the 19-year-old Marine.

Having apparently given up hope of being rescued, Rother finally set out to save his own life. Three times he set out arrow formations made of stones, revealing the direction of his flight for life through the California wasteland. When the 160 member search team eventually discovered his skeletal remains on December 4, it was clear just how nearly Rother had come to saving himself. His wallet, poncho, clothing and M203 rifle-grenade launcher were discovered; his body was not far away. Having covered nearly 17 miles through the treacherous terrain, Lance Corporal Rother died within one mile of old U.S. Route 66. In His final moments of life, delirious from heat exhaustion, Jason Rother took off his clothing and folded each piece neatly along with his poncho. Leaving his belongings in an orderly pile he then wandered a short distance to the place of his death. San Bernadino County Sheriff's Deputy Chief Jerome Ringhofer, who led the search team, said, "He made a heroic effort, and he almost succeeded . . . He had to see the highway. You can't miss it."[2]

The desert is a lonely and desperate place. Maybe that's why ascetics and criminals are about its only human inhabitants. David was neither, though he was being treated as the latter. The title of the psalm fixes the location from

which it arose, though not the exact time. It is possible
that this arose from the period of Saul's persecution of
David. It is more likely, however, to have arisen from David's
flight from his son Absalom's coup, since he refers to himself in the third person as "king" (v. 11). Though David
had been anointed for the throne when hunted by Saul,
he had not yet begun to rule.

*Have you ever been through a
spiritual desert? Have you ever
despaired over whether you'd
emerge again into the well-
watered life of God?*

What is certain is that
David was in flight for his life.
The desert had become his
only pathway of escape, but
the lonely landscape had become a metaphor for his barren heart and dry spirit. It was
a physical experience, but it
was the spiritual parallels that
frightened David most. If you've ever been through a spiritual desert you understand. Have you ever despaired over
whether you'd emerge again into the well-watered life of
God?

When David suddenly fled Jerusalem, he left behind
him the temple, the ark and everything Israel had known
about experiencing the manifest presence of God. He had
been robbed, not only of his kingdom, but of his intimacy
in worship with God. Now, however, in the desert he discovered that the intense spiritual desire within him could
become the doorway to rediscovering God's presence during a spiritual drought. David's prayer should wet your
appetite with hope that you too can emerge from the spiritual desert you may be in. When isolated in the desert,
David's yearning for God's presence brought him face to

face with his spiritual responsibilities as a worshiper. When you are dry spiritually, when you long for fresh intimacy with God, it is essential to rediscover your spiritual responsibilities as well.

Perpetual Seeking

Fresh intimacy with God requires a perpetual commitment to seeking him:

Psalm 63
A Psalm of David, when he was in the wilderness of Judah.

¹ O God, you are my God; earnestly I seek you;
my soul thirsts for you;
my flesh faints for you,
as in a dry and weary land where there is no water.

Threatened by the removal of his normal patterns and place of worship and the spiritual void created by the tragedy of Absalom's revolt, David recommitted himself to the ardent and consistent pursuit of God. The word translated "earnestly" is related to the Hebrew word for "dawn." This has suggested to some a translation of "early will I seek you" (KJV). The word has the more basic idea of eagerness of heart than the earliness of the hour. Though, of course, to seek God early would require a certain level of earnestness. If our hearts are truly eager, they may awaken our bodies well before other responsibilities press their demands upon us.

Such earnestness is likened to physical thirst. How much, do you suppose, Jason Rother wanted water in those closing hours of his life? Is there any corollary here to what is going on in your spiritual life? Some despair at this point, for the feeling of intensity is gone from their spiritual life. Don't fret. The recommitment is not to feeling thirsty, but to seeking a satisfaction to your thirst. This you can do even without the sensation of thirst.

David was in "a dry and weary land where there is no water." What his eyes saw and his throat felt, his spirit knew as well. Every soul that walks with God enters this stretch of road at some point. It is required in walking with God. God will lead you here if you walk with Him long enough. During these times we feel none of the joy or passion with which we once sought God. At the moment nothing feels natural, right, passionate or real. We must reactivate our wills to seek God—not because it feels good to do so, but because it is life to do so.

You may not feel like seeking God, but you must! The weariness and longing to lie down and sleep is the gravitational pull of death. It must be resisted at all costs.

If the psalm demonstrates anything, it is the discipline and zeal with which David sought God. This discipline and zeal must now be taken up as an act of the will to fire again the intensity of his heart after God. What is the first thing you want to do when dry spiritually? It is probably the last thing you feel like doing—reestablish the discipline of pursuing God. But that's the trouble, isn't it? It feels like nothing but discipline. It feels like dry, grinding work. What once ran automatically on the raw fuel of desire now must be fired by an act of the will. You may not feel like seeking God, but you must! Like the nearly frozen wanderer on the polar cap, the feeling of weariness and the longing to lie down and sleep is the gravitational pull of death. It must be resisted at all costs! For your spiritual survival you must set out again and find and enjoy God's fellowship.

Perpetual Praising

Fresh intimacy with God requires also a perpetual commitment to praising Him. David could remember days when worship was powerful, passionate and personal:

> *2 So I have looked upon you in the sanctuary,*
> *beholding your power and glory.*

At the moment, here in the desert, it was none of these things. Yet the recollection of fresher days moves him to commit to worship God, again, not because it feels right, but because it is life. Indeed it is better than life:

> *3 Because your steadfast love is better than life,*
> *my lips will praise you.*

Ponder that for a moment. Be honest, what is there that is better than life? Say you're enjoying your favorite meal, and it's cooked to perfection and served with elegance. Your palate savors every bite. Your taste buds cry with delight. Then, suddenly, the last bite goes down wrong and becomes an obstruction in your throat. In an instant that meal means nothing—breath means everything. Or say you're driving with your family on a dream vacation—make it in the mountains. All points of the compass offer awe-inspiring natural wonders. Your family members stare in wide-eyed astonishment. Fresh winds of joy and wonder blow through your soul. As you round the bend on a narrow highway clinging to the side of a naked cliff of unfathomable proportions, you hear a loud explosion and feel the car suddenly pull to the outside lane with amazing force. In an instant your dream vacation means nothing—regaining control of the car means everything to you and your family. Or imagine watching your son score the winning touchdown in the state championship football game as time expires on the clock. The rush of adrenaline and pride rising from some indefinable spot inside your gut is uncontrollable. However, just as your son crossed the goal line, the opposing team's middle linebacker flung him to the ground, driving his head into the turf. In the midst of the jubilation you notice your son lying motionless below his celebrating teammates. As they bring the backboard onto the field and the ambulance pulls slowly along the sidelines, football, touchdowns and state championships mean nothing—all that matters is life!

Try it again; honestly, what is better than life, really? David confessed, "I have found only one thing better than my next breath—the steadfast love of the God I serve." More than water in a desert. More than a breath to a suffocating man. More than life itself. Been there? In that place, forms of worship don't matter; only worship does. The tabernacle is not necessary; only God is. Jerusalem is optional, priests secondary, sacrifices nice, but not required. All that matters is God, His love and my response to it.

God designs and allows the dry times to take us to this place. When you make it there you'll say with David,

> *⁴ So I will bless you as long as I live;*
> *in your name I will lift up my hands.*

Get the connection? Because praise is better than life (v. 2), I will do it till I have no life-breath left within me. In essence David prayed, "I'll use my dying breath to offer you praise, O God!" A commitment to praise God, even when it doesn't feel easy or right, is the pathway to getting to the place where it does feel right and easy again:

> *A committment to praise God, even when it doesn't feel easy or right, is the pathway to getting to the place where it does feel right and easy again.*

> *⁵ My soul will be satisfied as with fat and rich food,*
> *and my mouth will praise you with joyful lips.*

Perpetually seek and praise God and the hunger and thirst (v. 1) will be replaced with satisfaction (v. 5).

Perpetual Meditating

Fresh intimacy with God requires also a perpetual commitment to meditating upon Him. David spoke to God about those times,

> *⁶ when I remember you upon my bed,*
> *and meditate on you in the watches of the night;*
> *⁷ for you have been my help,*
> *and in the shadow of your wings I will sing for joy.*

Remember what has just transpired in David's life,

where he is, who is after him, what he has lost, what will befall him should Absalom's army catch him. Despite all that the night of his flight from Absalom wrought, he prayed, "In peace I will both lie down and sleep; for you alone, O LORD, make me dwell in safety" (Ps. 4:8). The next morning he testified, "I lay down and slept; I woke again, for the LORD sustained me" (Ps. 3:5).

How does that work? How can a person experience that? The answer is here in Psalm 63: "I remember you *upon my bed*, and meditate on you *in the watches of the night*" (v. 6). The Hebrews divided the night hours into three watches: from sunset to ten o'clock, from ten o'clock to two o'clock, and from two o'clock to sunrise. Whenever David awakened in the night, regardless of the time, he disciplined himself to think upon God. When worry took his mind and body hostage, he dragged his thoughts back to God. When anxiety pumped up his adrenaline and kept his body from sleep, David diluted it with massive doses of God-thoughts. This worked because David had a good memory: "You have been my help" (v. 7). And so David could say, "In the shadow of your wings I will sing for joy" (v. 7).

Where was David sleeping these days? In the desert? In the dirt? As a fugitive? Yes, but also no. He was, by his own testimony, asleep "in the shadow of [God's] wings." David has already alluded to the tabernacle and worship there (v. 2). So too this line takes us back there. The tabernacle housed the ark, upon which sat the mercy set. The mercy seat had two cherubim molded into it at either end, their wings rising and spreading over the top of the ark. Between the wings of these cherubim is where God localized and manifested His glorious presence. When Zadok and the Levites had brought it to the fleeing David, he sent them back with it to the tabernacle in Jerusalem (2 Sam. 15:24–25). He knew the ark was no lucky charm to be manipulated for selfish purposes (see 1 Sam. 4:3). Even now, though physically removed from Jerusalem, tabernacle and ark, David found himself dwelling by faith in the very presence of God, overshadowed by Him, gathered near His side in safety and peace!

How did David arrive back at that place? Through the discipline of meditating on God. It required that he "remember" God (v. 6). Meditating means recalling the faithful acts of God experienced in the past and rehearsing them in one's mind. It also requires that we "meditate" upon God. The word comes from a verb meaning to mutter, growl or groan. It has the sense of repeating something over and over again under your breath, mulling it over in your mind. It is talking to yourself about what you've made your mind think upon. Meditation is dissection of a thought—taking it apart, examining its parts, pondering its meaning, wringing every significance from it. When we choose our thoughts and wrench every ounce of life from them, the rain clouds of blessing begin to form on the horizon of our thirsty souls.

> [8] *My soul clings to you;*
> *your right hand upholds me.*

Perpetual Clinging

Fresh intimacy with God requires also a perpetual commitment to clinging to Him. When David exclaimed, "My soul clings to you" (v. 8) he used a word that combines both the notion of following after and holding fast. For this reason the Authorized Version reads, "followeth hard after Thee." The word had been used to describe Ruth's love for her mother-in-law Naomi. After the husbands of Namoi, Ruth and Orpah die, Naomi determines to return to her homeland. She tells Ruth and Orpah to turn back and remain in their homeland of Moab. Orpah kissed her mother-in-law goodbye, "but Ruth clung to her" (Ruth 1:14). Same word. As Naomi tried to walk down the road to home, Ruth followed, clinging to her in tears. There is emotion, intensity and effort wrapped up in this word!

Why do we continue to pursue One whom we have already found? The longing heart knows the answer the logical mind cannot comprehend.

David, in the midst of spiritual drought, made a similar commitment: "My soul clings to you"! Is that the set of your soul?

We must know both what this means and what it doesn't mean. It doesn't mean that the security of my walk with God is in my hands. That rests squarely in God's hands: "Your right hand upholds me" (v. 8). God's omnipotent and everlasting arms are under us; this is our great assurance in dry and troubled times (Deut. 33:27). His keeping does not, however, absolve us from our commitment to cling to Him.

Why, we may ask, would a person continue to pursue One that they have already found? How are you to cling to One in whose arms you already rest? The longing heart knows the answer the logical mind cannot comprehend.

A.W. Tozer perhaps stated it as well as any:

> To have found God and still pursue Him is the soul's paradox of love. . . . We have been snared in a spurious logic which insists that if we have found Him, we need no more seek Him. This is set before us as the last word in orthodoxy, and it is taken for granted that no Bible-taught Christian ever believed otherwise. Thus the whole testimony of the worshiping, seeking, singing church on that subject is crisply set aside.[3]

Perpetual Resting

A skeptic may be saying, "All this talk of seeking, praising, meditating and clinging to God sounds fine, but what about the thousands of people armed to the teeth, out for blood and thundering down upon David?" While David had begun to catch sight of God again, he had not lost sight of his circumstances. It's just that he knew a fresh intimacy with God also required a perpetual commitment to resting in Him. He closed his prayer this way:

> *⁹ But those who seek to destroy my life*
> *   shall go down into the depths of the earth;*
> *¹⁰ they shall be given over to the power of the sword;*
> *   they shall be a portion for jackals.*
> *¹¹ But the king shall rejoice in God;*
> *   all who swear by him shall exult,*
> *   for the mouths of liars will be stopped.*

There is the faint watermark of an earlier, epic rebellion standing behind the close of David's prayer. The ominous prediction that his enemies "shall go down into the depths of the earth" is an echo of another legendary rebellion in Israel. When Moses led the people from Egypt to the promised land, Korah led a rebellion against him. To settle the rebellion Moses challenged the rebels to let God decide who was in the right.

And as soon as he had finished speaking all these words, the ground under them split apart. And the earth opened its mouth and swallowed them up, with their households and all the people who belonged to Korah and all their goods. So they and all that belonged to them went down alive into Sheol, and the earth closed over them, and they perished from the midst of the assembly. (Num. 16:31–33)

Hadn't David said the same thing when Shimei cursed him along the road out of Jerusalem (2 Sam. 16:12)? David was at rest. "Let God decide! I know my heart. He knows their motives." Can't you picture some of those who'd fled with David rising that next morning, muscles stiff from a night on the ground and snapping to full alert as soon as their eyes opened? They jump to their feet and search in every direction to assess their circumstances. Once they realize there is no imminent danger, someone notices that David is nowhere to be seen. They call his name. Nothing. They split up and scour the surrounding area. Finally one among the party rounds a hill and there he is, relaxing under a small bush with a contented look upon his face. "Sir," they say, trying to interrupt his preoccupation, "we've got to get moving!" They try again. "Sir!" No response. "Your majesty, please! What about the armies of Israel?"

Just one word rises from David's lips: "Alpo."

The confused servant screws up his face in confusion, "Alpo?"

"Yes," David replies. "Alpo. You know, dog food."

OK, not quite. Actually he said, "They shall be a portion for jackals" (v. 10).

Are you able to find a place of rest in what you can control (seeking God) and in what you can't (emotions, desire, security)? This rest isn't a feeling that comes over you but a decision you make within yourself. Praying through a spiritual desert involves making the decision to take up that which we are responsible for and letting go of that for which we are not.

There is, if we look carefully, an observable cycle to praying through a spiritual drought. We begin with a recognition of our need: "My soul thirsts for you" (v. 1). As we pray through there comes an initial satisfaction of that desire: "My soul will be satisfied" (v. 5). But if we refuse to be contented with just a taste of God and press on in prayer, the desire will return and will have grown in intensity: "My soul clings to you" (v. 8).

The Christian life is a perpetual cycle of desire . . . seeking . . . satisfaction . . . increased desire . . . more fervent seeking . . . ever deepening satisfaction . . . increased desire . . . even more fervent seeking . . .

Do you desire God? Do you despair that you do not desire Him more? Do you want to want Him more? Once, when I was going through a dry stretch in my walk with Christ, someone handed me a card which simply read: "If for any reason you cannot pray, relax. The desire to pray is already a prayer." Know that it is so. Know that He hears your cry long before you can even articulate it.

Praying Through

Before reading on, pray through the dryness of your own soul toward God. Follow the pattern of Psalm 63.

- Tell God how much you want to experience Him in a deeper, more authentic way. If that doesn't fit your heart's condition, tell God how much you want to want Him that way. Covenant with God regarding some specific, concrete disciplines you will undertake to pursue knowing Him more deeply.

- Worship God. Sing to Him. Praise Him for His attributes. Delineate His names. Lift up His glorious character. Do it daily. Set specific times to do nothing but pause and worship God for who He is. Ask nothing, offer praise.

- Tonight take one verse of Scripture with you to bed. Commit it to memory and use whatever time you have between your head hitting the pillow and your drifting off to sleep to dissect that verse. Ask every question of it imaginable. Turn it over in your mind. View it from every possible angle. Tear it apart and put it back together. Apply it to every relationship or circumstance in your life.

- Refuse to let go of God by surrendering these disciplines. Be tenacious about them. Let nothing drive them out of your life. Yet in all this know that your security rests in the fact that God holds you, not how tightly you hold to Him. Let Him decide between you and those who challenge you. Rest in His wisdom, providence and protection.

12

Praying Through Slander

DAVID SAT confused, despondent and vulnerable in the desert. He thought he could detect the distant but distinct sound of the rumor mill grinding out its grist. It was his own subjects, grinding out his name once again, making him the subject of their gossip. Old vendettas die hard. Saul's family just couldn't let go. The Benjamites had long been loyal to their favored son. While bitterness may go underground and lie dormant for a time, the root springs to life again with very little cultivation. Absalom's revolt was all the encouragement Saul's kinsmen needed to take up once again the public disinformation campaign against the son of Jesse.

During the days of his decline, Saul had deftly employed the grapevine in an attempt to discredit David. He knew how to play upon tribal loyalties. His public relations office knew the kind of information to float before a public that wanted to believe the best about the king they had begged God for. His fellow-tribesmen led the cheers and disseminated the distortions.

After Saul's death Abner had appealed to Benjamite blood in thrusting forth Ishbosheth, son of Saul, as Israel's next king instead of David. Even after Abner defected to

David, the house of Saul fought to retain the throne. Their gradual, grinding humiliation simmered on low boil for decades. The breezes of David's current adversity fanned old resentments to flame.

Even Mephibosheth, the grandson of Saul to whom David displayed such generosity, was plotting to wrestle the throne from the king, according to Mephibosheth's servant Ziba. (David would later learn that Ziba was lying, but at this point the king believed he had been betrayed.)

David lifted his calloused fingers to the back of his head and winced as he rubbed the lump. His mind replayed scenes of Saul's kinsman Shimei as he had met David along his evacuation route with curses and stones.

Will this never end?

Now the sons of Abiathar had come to him in the desert, as arranged, and reported the state of affairs in Jerusalem. "Cush," they said, "is leading the chorus of lies against you."

Cush? The king racked his brain trying to place the name with a face. *Cush?* No recognition came to him. But it didn't matter; he was a Benjamite—enough said.

Indeed more than enough was being said.[1]

·   ·   ·   ·   ·

Slander is a powerful weapon. So powerful, in fact, that those bent on harm find it hard not to take it up.

In the 1950s Florida had a Senator by the name of Claude Pepper. He was an outspoken liberal and was a key target for rabid conservatives in what became known as the McCarthy Era. In an age of hysteria over communism, Claude's opponent, George Smathers, nicknamed Claude "The Red Pepper"—insinuating that he was a closet communist. During the campaign the right-wing seemed bent on exposing the secret vices of Pepper. They claimed he was "a known extrovert," that his sister was a "thespian," and his brother "a practicing *homo sapien*." They reported that when Pepper went to college he "matriculated" and that before his marriage Pepper had "practiced celibacy."

Many of the constituents in Pepper's ward were poorly educated rural voters. Not understanding the verbiage of the campaign trail, they assumed the worst. Pepper lost the election and was disgraced publicly.

As both a political and spiritual leader, David knew well the destructive nature of slander. The power of slander lies not in its truthfulness but in its timing. Face it, slander sells. Those in places of leadership are especially vulnerable—it takes only one rumor to end your leadership, destroy your life and ruin your family. Truth need not apply, only scandal. How are you to pray then? What do you say to the Lord when slander is slung your way?

Psalm 7

A Shiggaion of David, which he sang to the Lord concerning the words of Cush, a Benjaminite.

> *1 O Lord my God, in you do I take refuge;*
> *save me from all my pursuers and deliver me,*
> *2 lest like a lion they tear my soul apart,*
> *rending it in pieces, with none to deliver.*

Psalm 7 is a prayer in the face of slander. The title tells us simply that it was prayed "concerning the words of Cush, a Benjaminite." It is obvious from the prayer itself that Cush laid some scandalous charge against David (vv. 3–5). Cush is not mentioned by name elsewhere in the Bible, and thus we don't know the exact circumstances from which his slander and this prayer arose. We can piece together, however, something of the events surrounding it.

Cush was "a Benjamite," a kinsman of Saul. It is possible that this arose from the time of Saul's persecution of David. Saul had been paranoid and played on the sympathies of his fellow tribesmen (e.g., 1 Sam. 22:6–10). The Benjamites may have been generally inclined to see David as a usurper of the throne. Twice David had opportunity to kill Saul, and twice he refused to touch the Lord's anointed. The first time he cried out to Saul, "Why do you listen to the words of men who say, 'Behold, David seeks your harm?'" (1 Sam. 24:9). The second time he lashed out, "If it is the LORD who has stirred you up against me, may he accept an offering, but if it is men, may they be cursed before the LORD" (1 Sam. 26:19).

This smoldering resentment of the tribe of Benjamin continued well past Saul's death and into David's reign. When David fled Jerusalem at the time of Absalom's coup, another Benjamite named Shimei showed up to cast his bitter curses on David (2 Sam. 16:5–9). Even after Absalom's revolt was put down, another Benjamite called for sedition and separation from David (2 Sam. 20:1). Neither of these individuals is the Cush of Psalm 7, but they do show us the cultural context in which he operated.

David knew well the pain of slander. That pain became

a prayer. This prayer was designated a "Shiggaion." Many of the musical terms of the psalter are disputed as to their meaning. Some experts, however, link this word to a root meaning "to wander" and say that it may refer to a "wild, passionate song, with rapid changes of rhythm."[2] The unsettled rhythm apparently matched the severity of David's emotions, stirred as they were by the false charges leveled against him. Because praying through slander can be a wild, emotional ride, the psalm defies easy division. It does, however, tell us a lot about what goes into praying through such unjust accusations.

See Yourself

When the sword of slander runs us through, all we know is what we feel, what we fear. Notice how often the word "my" shows up in the first half of David's prayer: "my God" (v. 1), "my soul" (v. 2), "my God," "my hands" (v. 3), "my friend" (v. 4), "my soul," "my life," "my glory" (v. 5), "my enemies" (v. 6), "my right-eousness" (v. 8), "my shield" (v. 10). Slander makes us self-absorbed. When an artery has been laid open, it's difficult not to be caught up in stopping the bleeding!

Slander makes us self-absorbed. When an artery has been laid open, it's difficult not to be caught up in stopping the bleeding.

It is easy for us to downplay the seriousness of someone else's slander, especially David's. We view him as untouch-able. There were, however, approximately eight years be-tween the time of Saul's death and the time David actu-ally reigned over all Israel. It had been a volatile time filled with posturing and power struggles, particularly from Saul's tribe. Well after David's coronation his reign was still a precarious one, vulnerable enough that his own son could steal the hearts of the people. It is easy for us to look at another beset by scandal and say, "Take it easy! It's no big deal! It's all going to blow over!" That's right, it's not a big deal because it's *their* life, not yours.

Make it your life and reputation and you would be self-absorbed too. You would discover personally how slander distorts our sight. It can make the slanderers look like lions. "O LORD my God, in you do I take refuge; save me from all my pursuers and deliver me, lest like a lion they tear my soul apart, rending it in pieces, with none to deliver" (vv. 1–2).

Not long ago while we entertained guests, I spotted our cat C.C. proudly trotting across the backyard with a chipmunk in her mouth. I raced over to take a look as she rounded the corner of the house, and all the children were in hot pursuit as well. When she saw me she dropped her prey. The chipmunk, still alive and terribly frightened, went into a terrified scamper, searching for anything that looked like cover. Denunciations and name-calling descended upon C.C. by all the children. In their eyes, she had gone instantly from our beloved pet to a bloodthirsty predator— something on par with an ax-murderer!

It only proves that given the right circumstances anyone can look more dangerous than they really are. David often used the imagery of lions in his prayers (e.g., Ps. 17:12; 22:13, 21; 35:17). It came, I suppose, from years in the pasturelands guarding his father's sheep. More than once he rescued them from the jaws of a lion (1 Sam. 17:34–36).

The pain of slander makes us self-absorbed, and the self-orientation can make our slanderers appear stronger than they are and their slander more ruinous than it actually is.

Self-absorption also distorts our view of ourselves, making us appear like saints. Listen to how David viewed himself.

> *³ O Lord my God, if I have done this,*
>   *if there is wrong in my hands,*
> *⁴ if I have repaid my friend with evil*
>   *or plundered my enemy without cause,*
> *⁵ let the enemy pursue my soul and overtake it,*
>   *and let him trample my life to the ground*
>   *and lay my glory in the dust. Selah*
>
> *⁶ Arise, O Lord, in your anger;*
>   *lift yourself up against the fury of my enemies;*
>   *awake for me; you have appointed a judgment.*
> *⁷ Let the assembly of the peoples be gathered about you;*
>   *over it return on high.*
>
> *⁸ The Lord judges the peoples;*
>   *judge me, O Lord, according to my righteousness*
>   *and according to the integrity that is in me.*
> *⁹ Oh, let the evil of the wicked come to an end,*
>   *and may you establish the righteous—*
> *you who test the minds and hearts,*
>   *O righteous God!*
> *¹⁰ My shield is with God,*
>   *who saves the upright in heart.*

Was David that pure? Was he as sinless as he made it

seem? Of course not. In fact, as we have seen, the entire
mess with Absalom was traceable back to his sin with
Bathsheba. David was likely innocent in the matter of
which Cush spoke, but he was not flawless before God.

How then can he make such
challenges as "Judge me, O
LORD, according to my righteousness and according to the
integrity that is in me"?
David's challenge was put in
a "if I . . . if I . . . if I . . . then
. . ." form. Basically David
prayed, "God, if I have
sinned, then may lightning strike me down!"

*The challenge of praying
through slander is to first pray
through to the place where
you see yourself for who
you really are.*

The challenge of praying through slander is to first pray
through to the place where you see yourself for who you
really are. David was processing through to such a view of
himself.

See Your Savior

Amid the pain of lies, we must also pray through to the
place where we see our Savior for who He is. A transition
takes place in verse 10. The adrenaline rush of panic has
been spilled (vv. 1–9). Now David is not so self-absorbed.
He is in a place where he can get his eyes off himself and
see God more clearly. He began to see that God is *a God of
faithful keeping*. He prayed, "My shield is with God" (v. 10).
David often referred to God as his shield, surrounding him
from harm (e.g., Ps. 3:3; 5:12; 18:2, 30, 35; 28:7).

> *¹¹ God is a righteous judge,*
> *and a God who feels indignation every day.*

He also began to remember that God is *a God of judgment*: "God is a righteous judge." God is going to get this right. Things are not out of control—perhaps out of *my* control, but not out of total control. God will not be fooled. He can't be convinced. He knows the facts. He knows my heart. God is a God of righteous judgment. Pray through till you know that deep in your soul.

God is also *a God of swift wrath*, "a God who feels indignation every day." When His sovereign purposes have been served—and God won't waste a moment—He will bring to an end the injustice that has befallen you. Not a day passes but what God doesn't act in judgment upon someone perpetrating injustice upon the innocent. We don't always see His silent servants as they carry out His verdict and exact His justice, but they are dispatched daily and do their job exceedingly well. "The wrath of God *is being revealed* from heaven against all the godlessness and wickedness of men who suppress the truth by their wickedness" (Rom. 1:18, NIV). We, like David, want judgment to fall *now* ("Arise, O LORD . . . lift yourself up . . . awake," v. 6)[3] but He daily dispenses His justice according to His sovereign purposes.

Know in your heart that God can immediately put an end to the rumor mill that is grinding out your name. You don't have to wait for a court date, for the attorneys to collect their evidence or for a jury to be selected. A trial doesn't have to unfold and a verdict be reached. God is just as swift in justice as His purposes allow.

God will utterly destroy sin and the sinners who perform it:

> *¹² If a man does not repent, God will whet his sword;*
> *he has bent and readied his bow;*
> *¹³ he has prepared for him his deadly weapons,*
> *making his arrows fiery shafts.*

Strong words, but our business is to see Him as He is
and to trust Him to be Himself. Revenge is God's, not ours
(Rom. 12:19). Praying through requires seeing God for who
He is and letting Him do what only He can do. Praying
through means letting go of vendettas, even while we cling
tenaciously to God as our Vindicator. A tough balance to
maintain, one only attainable when we've prayed through
the pain and into a clear view of God. We've already noted
George Herbert's wise comment, but it's worth a second
look: "Living well is the best revenge."

See the Slander

As David's soul began to settle and his heart rest in God,
he was able to see not only himself for who he was and
God for who He is, but the slander for what it is. We must
pray through to the same insight. When we do, we'll notice that *slander is like a birth.*

> *¹⁴ Behold, the wicked man conceives evil*
> *and is pregnant with mischief*
> *and gives birth to lies.*

Children ask their parents, "Where do babies come

from?" When slander strikes home the naive ask God, "Where did this mess come from?" Slander is birthed from an evil heart. First there is a conception and it arises from "evil." Someone is mad at someone else. They want to pay back. A juicy bit of infor-mation is leaked with a cas-ual slip of the tongue. A monster is conceived in the womb of public opinion. Then comes the pregnancy and the baby's name is "mischief." The evil of the heart has now become active ill-will. Soon enough

Slander has a built-in self-judgment. The slander consumes the slanderer. Like a hunter who sets a trap and only succeeds in snaring himself, the slanderer will fall victim to his own lies.

there is a birth—a big, fat, bounding bundle of "lies" has been birthed into the world!

A tiny indulgence conceived in a moment of self-pity has given birth to a monster now consuming its victim. A single lie takes on a life of its own and grows into a mon-strosity. Isn't this the oft-repeated pattern of all sin? "Each person is tempted when he is lured and enticed by his own desire. Then desire when it has conceived gives birth to sin, and sin when it is fully grown brings forth death" (James 1:14–15).

As we pray through, our improved sight will also reveal that *slander is like a trap*:

> ¹⁵ *He makes a pit, digging it out,*
> *and falls into the hole that he has made.*

While the pain of slander is fresh we might not see it, but down the road, having prayed through, we will see

that slander has built into it a self-judging verdict. The
slander consumes the slanderer. Like a hunter who digs
out a pit, covers it over to trap his prey and only succeeds
in snaring himself, so too the slanderer will fall victim to
his own lies.

Sir Robert Watson Watt was the inventor of radar technology. Years after his discovery he was caught in a speed
trap in Canada. After receiving his ticket he wrote this
ironic ditty:

> Pity Sir Robert Watson Watt,
> Strange target of his radar plot,
> And this, with others I could mention,
> A victim of his own invention.

Slanderers are inventors. They produce lies that destroy.
They will, however, end up destroying only themselves.
Pray through until you can rest in this knowledge.

Indeed when we pray through to a clearer vision of the
slander we face, we will discover that *slander is like a boomerang.*[4]

> *16 His mischief returns upon his own head,*
> *and on his own skull his violence descends.*

There is a reciprocating judgment built into sin. How
well I remember my cousin Mark's boomerang crashing
through Mr. Reinburger's front window—after we'd been
carefully instructed not to throw it in the front yard! Your
sins will find you out. Pray through till you know this is
true for those who sin by slandering you.

Praying through slander requires seeing yourself for who

you are, God for who He is and the slander for what it is. But how do you know when you've really prayed through to that point? When we honestly utter the last words of David's prayer:

> *17 I will give to the LORD the thanks due to his righteousness,*
>   *and I will sing praise to the name of the LORD, the Most High.*

Easy? Never! Possible? Yes. Consider this observation by James Montgomery Boice:

> The seventh psalm is a great testimony. Yet here is the striking thing. It is uttered at a time when, so far as we know, David had not yet obtained the earthly justice from God that he was seeking. He had come to God with his problem, which was the right and wise thing to do. In doing so, he has provided us with an example of what we can do in similar circumstances. Yet in spite of these many right attitudes and actions we do not know if David was actually vindicated in this life.[5]

Remember, gratitude never has to wait for deliverance to arrive, for its lifeblood is faith and its heartbeat is prayer.

Praying Through

When the pain of slander pierces your heart, pray through to a place of rest in God's keeping. Use Psalm 7 as your guide:

- Begin by admitting to God the nearly complete self-absorption you are experiencing. Confess your fears and tell Him how your slanderers appear to you.

Admit that they are likely not as evil as you think and that you are not as righteous as you'd like to believe.

- Having thoroughly explored your worries and fears before God, now resolutely set your eyes upon Him. Take Him as your shield. Affirm the righteousness of His judgments and the perfection of His timing. Freely express your dismay at what may seem His lack of response, but admit that you lack the fuller perspective to pronounce the righteous judgment required. Write out a covenant with God to not take your own vengeance. Leave your slanderers with God.

- Tell God that you trust Him to straighten out the lies about you that have been birthed. Affirm to God that He has built into slander a self-judging mechanism that will come back on the heads of the liars. Articulate to Him your trust and ask for patience to await His verdict.

- Finally, turn to God in prayers of thanksgiving. Praise Him for His perfect righteousness. Worship Him as "the LORD, the Most High," the God who keeps covenant with His own and who stands over them as their Protector. Express your gratitude for His faithful keeping, even when the danger still feels imminent and unresolved.

13

Praying Through Yesterday

LISTEN TO THAT! It's the sound of peace. Kids chattering at play in the streets below. Women clanking pots as they putter around their fires. The elders sitting at the city gate solving a dispute about a boundary stone between two farmers. An old woman scolding her husband for picking at the beginning of the evening meal. It's the sound of life, the good life, the life God promised.

David sits, chin resting in his hands, lazily gazing out over his city. The silver in his beard shimmers in the sun of early evening. The long shadows, the warm glow, the serenity—it all seems to make time stand still for a few moments, and David soaks in the thoughtful silence. *Shalom*—it's the only word to describe it. Peace, wholeness, security, blessing. *Shalom.*

Hand-to-hand combat with a lion and bear? David smiles and shakes his head. *Goliath who?* Surely that was another lifetime. The days of panicked flight from Saul seem but a foggy memory, as if read from the musty scroll of some epic hero, but certainly not descriptive of something he's lived. Gone are the incessant wars, the bloody battles, the saber-rattling of wanna-be kings and the raids on boarder towns by the Philistines. The bitter antipathy of the

Benjamites is but a foggy memory. The scars from poor choices remain, but their sting is gone under the balm of grace. The Absalom-ache continues, but the sharp stabs of responsibility and regret have matured into a settled wisdom.

It's been a long road and quite a ride, but the drama now has given way to realization of the dream. As David soaks in the warmth of the setting sun and surveys the life that is his, an impression tumbles through the conscious thoughts of his mind: *This is what it's like to live inside a promise.* And then a second, even more powerful realization: *And to think, it's only just begun!*[1]

· · · · ·

What would you like your last prayer to be like? Praying in youth is one thing. In those days *tomorrow* looms large. But by now you've prayed through many of life's problems as much of *tomorrow* has become *today* and passed into *yesterday*. What about that last prayer you'll ever utter? How sad *tomorrow* can appear when suddenly we realize it has become *yesterday*!

Today is the time to prepare to pray through *yesterday*. Hear the musing of this now anonymous British lad.

> What shall I think when I am called to die?
> Shall I not find too soon my life has ended
> The years, too quickly, have hastened by
> With so little done of all that I intended.
> There were so many things I'd meant to try,
> So many contests I'd hope to win;
> And lo, the end approaches just as I
> Was thinking of preparing to begin.[2]

The wise prepare to pray through *yesterday*. It takes a lifetime to prepare to pray through the end of life. Psalm 18 is such a prayer. In this prayer we listen to David pray through his yesterdays. It gathers up a lifetime of praying through the problems of life and offers that life back up in prayer to God. David was not sinless nor was his life void of regret, but he was able to pray through to a place of grace and rest with yesterday. Psalm 18 is, in essence, a photo album of David's memories. You may take note that out of a life filled with problems that have moved him to prayer, David now prays the first and only of these four-teen historical psalms from a positive experience. Grati-tude drips from his lips as he prays over a lifetime of pray-ing through. Note where the prayer begins:

Psalm 18

To the choirmaster. A Psalm of David, the servant of the Lord, who addressed the words of this song to the Lord on the day when the Lord rescued him from the hand of all his enemies, and from the hand of Saul. He said:

1 I love you, O Lord, my strength.

Not only does the first line tell you the power of praying through life's problems, it is the only time this verb is used to describe man's love for God.[3] It is a deeply emotional term, full of compassion and pathos. This prayer is not a

The prayer of Psalm 18 is not a forced act of the will to trust God; it is the overflow of a life saturated with the goodness of God.

forced act of the will to trust God; it is the overflow of a life saturated with the goodness of God.

How can I finish like that? How can I come to love God so deeply? David's prayer suggests five keys to preparing to pray through yesterday.[4] Pray through till these are part of the fabric of your life, and you'll be prepared for the last prayer you may ever utter.

Aim to Know God

The opening words of David's prayer reveal how deeply he had come to know God as he had prayed through the passages of his life. Notice the eight names or titles of God he stacks one upon another as he praises the God he's come to know:[5]

> [2] *The LORD is my rock and my fortress and my deliverer,*
> *my God, my rock, in whom I take refuge,*
> *my shield, and the horn of my salvation, my stronghold.*
> [3] *I call upon the LORD, who is worthy to be praised,*
> *and I am saved from my enemies.*

It is as though David shuffles one snapshot after another before us in an effort to show how this glorious God has proven Himself in his life. It's almost as though David motions for us to lean in close as he says, "Here is God and me when He delivered me from the lion and the bear. And, oh, look! Here is God and me when He rescued me from the clutches of Saul! And here is God and me when He . . ." Get the picture? Every title—whether rock, fortress, deliverer, refuge, shield, horn of salvation or stronghold—pointed to a specific time when God had in specific ways met David in his hour of need. Throughout the entire psalm, David uses twelve different titles for God and employs them in speaking thirty-four different times about God.

One of the greatest compliments you can pay a person is to use his or her name when you address them. When someone uses my first name while talking with me, it tells me he knows me, respects me and feels free with me. Using a person's name is one of the best ways to honor him and to endear him to you. David, after years of walking with God and seeing Him deliver him repeatedly, had marshaled a vast array of names and titles for God. David knew God by name. Indeed, by name*s*! Every one of them expresses some different quality of God's character and person.

How are we to assess if we know God by name? This is more than, "Do I know God?" And it goes beyond, "What can I recount about God?" No, we each must ask, "Do I know God *by name*? From experience?"

When our youngest child, a son, was born to us, we decided to name him after his two grandfathers. Clinton Dean. Clinton from Clinton Elwood Patterson—his maternal grandfather and Dean from Forest Dean Kitchen—my father. If we were to name him after both grandfathers it had to be either Clinton Dean or Forest Elwood. We decided that the latter would be just too much timber. He'd probably have ended up as Woody. So, Clinton Dean it was and is. The thing is, the only person I'd really known personally by the name of Clint was my father-in-law. Now my tiny son was in my arms, and I was calling him by that name. That name had been associated—wonderfully, I might add—with Julie's father. At first it seemed funny saying it in soft tones and a baby voice as I coddled my son. All my experience associated with the name said these new actions were odd. But now, nine years later, as I call my son Clint by name, the vast majority of the experience associated with the name arises from that relationship. It is the most natural and wonderful thing in the world to call him by his first name!

Have you put yourself in situations where God must be God if you are to survive and go on with Him? Then you are truly getting to know God.

That is how names are. They gain personal significance through experience. When naming our children I'd raise a possibility, and my wife would occasionally wrinkle her nose and say, "No. Just won't work. I knew a strange kid in third grade by that name. Just won't work." From time to time the same thing happened when she suggested a name to me. You see, names acquire significance based upon personal experience.

Have you, through enduring obedience to God, put yourself in situations where God must be God if you are to survive and go on for Him? Have you so walked with God that you can say with David, "I call upon the LORD, who is worthy to be praised, and I am saved from my enemies" (v. 3)? That is how you learn to know God by name. When you find yourself in a place where God must show up and be your fortress (or refuge or shield or rock, take your pick), you cry out to God and He proves in your experience to be just that, then you are truly getting to know

God. Make such knowledge of God your aim. Pray through life till you are getting to know Him by experience.

Aim to Walk with God

Such praying and living might also be known as walking with God. As we turn the page of David's photo album, we find him remembering some of the terrible tight spots that walking with God had put Him in. Listen to him rehearse those times and confess his need:

> *4 The cords of death encompassed me;*
> *   the torrents of destruction assailed me;*
> *5 the cords of Sheol entangled me;*
> *   the snares of death confronted me.*
>
> *6 In my distress I called upon the LORD;*
> *   to my God I cried for help.*
> *From his temple he heard my voice,*
> *   and my cry to him reached his ears.*

What do you do when you are in that kind of trouble? Where do you look? David looked to the God he walked with. But why? What makes a person in such dire circumstances believe that God is really with them at all? Because God had established a track record of delivering those who trust Him. Here is what I mean. Take a moment and glance over verses 7–15. You'll discover some powerful imagery. It recalls two of God's greatest deliverances in Israel's history: Moses meeting God on Mount Sinai (vv. 7–12) and Moses and the people of Israel at the Red Sea (vv. 13–15).

> [7] *Then the earth reeled and rocked;*
>> *the foundations also of the mountains trembled*
>> *and quaked, because he was angry.*
> [8] *Smoke went up from his nostrils,*
>> *and devouring fire from his mouth;*
>> *glowing coals flamed forth from him.*
> [9] *He bowed the heavens and came down;*
>> *thick darkness was under his feet.*
> [10] *He rode on a cherub and flew;*
>> *he came swiftly on the wings of the wind.*
> [11] *He made darkness his covering, his canopy around him,*
>> *thick clouds dark with water.*
> [12] *Out of the brightness before him*
>> *hailstones and coals of fire broke through his clouds.*
>
> [13] *The LORD also thundered in the heavens,*
>> *and the Most High uttered his voice,*
>> *hailstones and coals of fire.*
> [14] *And he sent out his arrows and scattered them;*
>> *he flashed forth lightnings and routed them.*
> [15] *Then the channels of the sea were seen,*
>> *and the foundations of the world were laid bare*
> *at your rebuke, O LORD,*
>> *at the blast of the breath of your nostrils.*

"But," you object, "that wasn't David's experience. That was something that happened hundreds of years prior to his birth. It was just a story to him, like much of the Bible is to me. Inspiring, perhaps, but it isn't my story!" Oh, but it was his story, and it can be yours as well.

David was looking over the experiences of his life—a life spent walking with God—and he could say, "Look what God has done for me! Just as God manifested Himself on behalf of Moses and the Israelites of old when they were walking in His way, so too He has manifested Himself on my behalf when I have walked in His ways!" The God of the universe is not a detached, disinterested Deity, but the living God who is actively involved in the everyday affairs of people who make His will their own and prove it through obedience.

> *The living God is actively involved in the everyday affairs of people who make His will their own and prove it through obedience.*

Look at God's record: those who take on His will, walk in His way, care for His concerns, join Him in what He is doing—these people experience His power. That was David's testimony.

> ^{16} *He sent from on high, he took me;*
>   *he drew me out of many waters.*
> ^{17} *He rescued me from my strong enemy*
>   *and from those who hated me,*
>   *for they were too mighty for me.*
> ^{18} *They confronted me in the day of my calamity,*
>   *but the LORD was my support.*
> ^{19} *He brought me out into a broad place;*
>   *he rescued me, because he delighted in me.*

Notice carefully the verbs: "He sent . . . he took me . . . he drew me out . . . He rescued me . . . he brought me out . . . he rescued me . . . he delighted in me."

"God never does anything like that for me," you complain. What are you asking Him to do? Walk with you? Or are you walking with Him? It is in the circle of His will that He pours out His power. All who live within the circle of His will experience the downpour of His power. It is futile and arrogant to go your way, asking God to bless your plans and expect that He will manifest His power on your behalf. God exists first, not to bestow blessings, but to be obeyed. In the path of obedience His blessing is unfailingly found.

Aim to Honor God

Read the next lines of David's prayer, but before you do, I must warn you. What you are about to read may be unsettling. In fact, it sounds arrogant.

> **20** *The Lord dealt with me according to my righteousness;*
> *according to the cleanness of my hands he rewarded me.*
> **21** *For I have kept the ways of the Lord,*
> *and have not wickedly departed from my God.*
> **22** *For all his rules were before me,*
> *and his statutes I did not put away from me.*
> **23** *I was blameless before him,*
> *and I kept myself from my guilt.*
> **24** *So the Lord has rewarded me according to my righteousness,*
> *according to the cleanness of my hands in his sight.*

To our ears that smacks of spiritual pride. Trouble is we don't hear them in their original context. David was not speaking of his own spiritual perfection, but was giving an honest summation of the general intent of his heart throughout life. He was simply saying, "I have been faithful to God. Perfect? No, of course not! But the broad course of my life reveals that I have, even after I sinned, come back to the purposes of God and pursued Him."

It is precisely because of the perceived tone of these verses that some feel this psalm had to have been written early in David's life, and was only later added by an editor into 2 Samuel 22. The reasoning goes something like this: How could David be so presumptuous as to boast of his purity after the fiasco with Bathsheba and after experiencing the devastation that came from sinfully neglecting his family? It is possible that this was written earlier in David's life, but could a man of "lesser" sins have justly prayed this way? The better option is to see that when God chose David to be king, He knew not only his past but also his future, and He still called him a man after His own heart (1 Sam. 13:14). Perfect? Hardly. But a man who consistently came back again and again to that which was, and is, first upon God's heart. David was simply asserting his enduring desire to honor God.

Keep that in mind as you listen in to the next lines of his prayer.

> ²⁵ *With the merciful you show yourself merciful;*
> *with the blameless man you show yourself blameless;*
> ²⁶ *with the purified you show yourself pure;*
> *and with the crooked you make yourself seem tortuous.*
> ²⁷ *For you save a humble people,*
> *but the haughty eyes you bring down.*
> ²⁸ *For it is you who light my lamp;*
> *the Lord my God lightens my darkness.*
> ²⁹ *For by you I can run against a troop,*
> *and by my God I can leap over a wall.*
> ³⁰ *This God—his way is perfect; the word of the Lord proves true;*
> *he is a shield for all those who take refuge in him.*

Put verses 20–24 together with verses 25–30; you'll discover that what we have are not the arrogant boasts of a self-satisfied man, but an enduring principle of life with God: *God deals with us as we deal with Him.* When I am faithful to God, God is faithful to me. When I work for God, God works on my behalf. When I walk with God, God walks with me. When I honor God, God honors me.

This was the principle long before David showed up on the scene: "Those who honor me I will honor, and those who despise me shall be lightly esteemed" (1 Sam. 2:30). It endured throughout his lifetime (2 Sam. 22:26–28). Jesus affirmed it: "If anyone serves me, the Father will honor him" (John 12:26) and it is still true today: "Draw near to God, and he will draw near to you" (James 4:8).

God will deal with you as you deal with Him. This is not works righteousness. It is an affirmation that only those who trust and obey experience God's grace.

God will deal with you as you deal with Him. This is not works righteousness. It is an affirmation that only the believing (and trust and obedience always go together) experience God's grace.

"But I'm no David!" Exactly! That is why the fourth key for preparing to pray through yesterday is to aim to depend upon God.

Aim to Depend Upon God

As David stood upon the mountain he had been ascending all his life, he looked back into the valley and reviewed where God's path had led him. Looking back, David recounted again the faithfulness of God. Read his recollections in verses 31–45, and as you do, see if you can count how many times the personal pronouns "I," "me" or "my" show up.

³¹ *For who is God, but the* L<small>ORD</small>*?*
  And who is a rock, except our God?—
³² *the God who equipped me with strength*
  and made my way blameless.
³³ *He made my feet like the feet of a deer*
  and set me secure on the heights.
³⁴ *He trains my hands for war,*
  so that my arms can bend a bow of bronze.
³⁵ *You have given me the shield of your salvation,*
  and your right hand supported me,
  and your gentleness made me great.
³⁶ *You gave a wide place for my steps under me,*
  and my feet did not slip.
³⁷ *I pursued my enemies and overtook them,*
  and did not turn back till they were consumed.
³⁸ *I thrust them through, so that they were not able to rise;*
  they fell under my feet.
³⁹ *For you equipped me with strength for the battle;*
  you made those who rise against me sink under me.
⁴⁰ *You made my enemies turn their backs to me,*
  and those who hated me I destroyed.
⁴¹ *They cried for help, but there was none to save;*
  they cried to the L<small>ORD</small>*, but he did not answer them.*
⁴² *I beat them fine as dust before the wind;*
  I cast them out like the mire of the streets.

⁴³ *You delivered me from strife with the people;*
  you made me the head of the nations;
  people whom I had not known served me.

> *44 As soon as they heard of me they obeyed me;*
> *foreigners came cringing to me.*
> *45 Foreigners lost heart*
> *and came trembling out of their fortresses.*

Did you do it? If you read carefully you found them used thirty-two times! Sounds pretty self-absorbed! But strangely I'm not left with the feeling that David was fixated upon himself. I'm left more impressed with God than with David. Perhaps that is because fifteen times David recounted what God had done for him (fifty-nine in the entire psalm!). Hans Wilhelm Hertzberg, in commenting on the same text in 2 Samuel 22, is perceptive:

> David's history could have been narrated as that of a great and powerful king.
> *This chapter, however, is concerned that it should be understood as the action of a great and powerful God.*[6]

Actually, what we hear in these verses is simply the same deliverance spoken of in verses 4–19, but from a different perspective. Whereas here the majority of the references are to David (I, me, or my), there the names of God or pronouns referring to Him were found twenty-six times. Same event, different perspective—one divinely oriented, the other personally oriented.[7]

Here is what David was saying: In the outflow of life, God works through me. If God's work is going to be done, God is going to have to do it. I can no more perform the work of God than I could lift the earth. But God, by issuing His commands, declares me responsible to do His will. God requires the impossible of me.

Know that feeling?

Relax, here's the principle: *I take responsibility; God takes the load.* I must step out in obedience to the commands of God, fully knowing that if God doesn't demonstrate His power in me, I'm sunk and His will won't be accomplished. But God calls me to step out and responsibly undertake to do His will. As I step out in this way, I am counting on His power. The fun begins when God does extend His power and His work is done and He is glorified in my weakness. As He does His work through me, the glory goes to Him because it is obvious that I could not do what God has done through me.

> *I must step out in obedience to the commands of God, fully knowing that if God doesn't demonstrate His power in me, I'm sunk!*

> **46** *The LORD lives, and blessed be my rock,*
> *and exalted be the God of my salvation—*
> **47** *the God who gave me vengeance*
> *and subdued peoples under me,*
> **48** *who delivered me from my enemies;*
> *yes, you exalted me above those who rose against me;*
> *you rescued me from the man of violence.*

> **49** *For this I will praise you, O LORD, among the nations,*
> *and sing to your name.*
> **50** *Great salvation he brings to his king,*
> *and shows steadfast love to his anointed,*
> *to David and his offspring forever.*

Aim to Wait on God

Clearly this psalm is David's, and it surveys his life of walking with God. Yet ultimately the prayer is about someone else—Jesus Christ. This is a wonderfully messianic prayer. David knew that his past was a key part of a glorious future. His life mattered; it was connected to something beyond it, and he was willing to wait on God for the ultimate purpose of his life to unfold.

When the psalm title designated David as "the servant of the LORD," it employed a rarely used title with powerful significance. That title was used twice of Joshua (e.g., Josh. 24:29). It occurs also in reference to Moses (e.g., Deut. 34:5) and is used to point forward to the coming Messiah (e.g., Isa. 40ff).[8] This was a way of saying that what God had been doing when He brought His people out of Egypt through Moses to form a nation, and what He had done when He brought them into the land of promise through Joshua, this He was still doing through David's life. What God had been up to through Moses, Joshua and now David would only find its ultimate fulfillment in the ultimate "servant of the LORD," Jesus Christ.

In fact the next to last verse (v. 49) of this psalm was picked up by the Apostle Paul and quoted in Romans 15:9. It was used there as evidence that God has always been interested in reaching not only His chosen people Israel, but all the peoples of the earth. Paul declares that God has made provision for this salvation through the sending and the sacrifice of Jesus Christ, the descendant of David.

The final verse speaks of God's love for "his anointed" (v. 50). Surely this designated David. Yet it is instructive to know that the term is one from which we get the term "Messiah." And the final breath of David's prayer speaks of God's unfailing love to "David and his offspring forever." The term "offspring" is singular. Read in light of the New Testament's revelation, this is clearly a prophetic signpost pointing forward to the one singular and ultimate King, the King of kings, who would finally and forever sit upon the throne of David—Jesus Christ, our Lord. Indeed the victories David celebrated here had not been given merely for his sake, but for the sake of the redemptive plan of God that would find its crescendo in Jesus Christ. As David drew his prayer to a close, he naturally shifted from the first person ("I," v. 49) to the third person ("his king" and "his anointed," v. 50), realizing that the significance of his life lay not behind him, but before him—in the promise of his Greater Son.

David looked back over a lifetime of walking with God and gave thanks for His abundant grace. He was able to do so because he could also look forward and see that his life would find its ultimate significance in things yet to unfold—things for which he was willing to wait even beyond this lifetime. From our vantage point we can see that David's life was wrapped up in Jesus Christ. He looked forward in faith to Him. We look backward in faith at what He has done, yet also forward, like David, waiting for the final fulfillment of all God's purposes and promises in Christ. Make it your aim to let all things be resolved in that future time.

What kind of prayer would you like to close your life with? How do you want to pray through yesterday?

As I mentioned before, this is the only one of these historically-footnoted psalms that has arisen from positive circumstances. It reminds us that while life is a struggle, God's grace can enable us to look back upon it as a sweet experience.

This seems the perfect place to have wrapped up these prayers, yet there remains one more psalm to be prayed through. It sounds a much needed warning as we pray our way through the passages of life.

Praying Through

Set apart an extended period of time to prepare for praying through an entire lifetime of walking with God. Use Psalm 18 as the guide for your communion with God.

- Ask God to let you know Him deeply, personally, in your experience. Ask Him to reveal in your experience the greatness of who He is.

- Determine that you will walk with God. Ask God to forgive you for demanding that He walk with you, rather than pledging that you'll walk with Him. Petition God for the joy of simply knowing His presence at each moment of your life.

- Ask God to cleanse your heart from anything as yet unresolved from your past. Make restitution. Seek forgiveness from all He guides you to. No matter how badly you have failed, come back to God and purpose to make His honor your only goal. Ask God to impart to your heart a pure desire for His glory alone.

- Ask God to show you the next step along life's path. Take it, no matter how impossible obedience may appear. Trust God to take the load when you take the responsibility of obedience. Move out. Don't just pray, obey!

- Finally, prayerfully covenant to wait upon God for the ultimate meaning and outcome of your life. Entrust your life, its meaning and its purpose, to Jesus Christ. Refuse to take up anything other than God's purposes as revealed in Christ. Rest in the knowledge that the greater portion of your life's meaning will be visible only in the rearview mirror.

14

Praying Through the Finish Line

I WONDER. Things had been slow lately. Good, but slow. No, make that great. For a long time. But even "great" can be boring. No battles to occupy the mind with military strategy. No great affairs of state. No major domestic issues demanding creative problem solving. Everything was secure. Had been for years.

David's mind had been wandering of late. Free time had tempted him to start listening to the stories, the legends told around evening fires and whispered by folk with adoring glances as his retinue passed by. Then a velvety voice spoke from within. It came so naturally it almost seemed his own, if it wasn't for a hissing sound at the end of each sentence: *Are they right? Just how great am I?*

It all blossomed in that time of life when it's easy to begin wondering about the legacy you'll leave. A man wants to measure the difference he's made. Who is he? How will he be remembered?

Then one afternoon, while reclining on the balcony of his palace with servants waving palm fronds over him to lessen the late summer's heat, a revelation came. It made so much sense! Of course, it was the perfect standard of measure. His greatest contribution to the nation, humanly speaking, had been expanding and securing its borders, conciliating contrarians and defeating its foes. He was a military man, start to finish. What better measure of his greatness than a detailed accounting of his military might?

David wasted no time in summoning General Joab. *Number the troops?* Even backstabbing Joab begged the king to reconsider. Such self-glorying would surely not stand unnoticed by the God who will not share His glory with another. But kings trump generals. For nearly ten months David wrung his hands, counted in his head and lay awake at night wondering aloud to himself with possible estimations of the measure of his greatness. Just what would the final tally reveal?

At last the reluctant general appeared once again before his commander-in-chief. The news was more than even David had dreamed: He had amassed a standing army of 1.3 million men!

But before the door had slammed behind Joab, a minor chord sounded in the king's heart. He knew this messenger well; the hammer of guilt had struck the chord of conscience. That old familiar dissonance was disconcerting. The note continued to sound throughout the night. The dawn brought the announcement that Gad, David's faithful court prophet, wished for an audience with the king. The look on David's face told Gad that God's message had preceded the prophet. His was but to deliver the options: "Three years of famine, three months of fleeing from your enemies, or three days of plague throughout the land—pick your poison."[1]

· · · · ·

Run *through* the finish line. Not *to* the finish line, but *through* it! That's the most basic rule of racing. Elementary. Fundamental. Unquestionable. I learned it early, and I learned it often as a track athlete in junior and senior high school.

It was a crisp, beautiful spring afternoon. I adjusted the blocks, got down into them and, pausing for a moment, then sprang into a full sprint, sustained it for about fifteen yards and then circled back to wait for the starter to call us to the line.

"Runners take your marks!" the command came. As I'd done countless times before, I settled into the blocks, focused my mind, stared at the cinders directly below my nose and drew a few deep, steady breaths. "On your mark!" Pause—that tense, interminable pause—"crack!" the gun sounded. All eight runners broke from the line in synchronized fury and began the swift journey to the finish line. It quickly became a typical race for me. I had made it safely through the prelims and into the final. Now I was well ahead of middle of the pack, but obviously not able to overtake the first-place runner. It looked like I would take third place again. Not bad. No, not great, but respectable. I had other races to run that night, so somewhere in the back of my brain, I began to shut down ever so slightly, reasoning that I'd collect my third-place medal and conserve my energies for perhaps a better showing in the night's later races.

I crossed the line, coasted briefly to a stop and started a slow walk down the track to cool down. I was quickly approached by the spotter assigned to my lane. She was uttering some gibberish and pointing in animated fashion at a point back down the track. When I finally tuned into her speech, I heard her say, "You stopped too soon! You didn't run through the finish line." I whirled to look behind me and realized my error. I'd mistaken one of the many other markings on the track for the finish line of *this* race. I had slowed down too soon . . . and been passed by the other five runners. I had finished dead last!

_____ ⌒ _____

When you are preoccupied with secondary matters, it is easy to mistake the finish line and end up dead last.

When you are preoccupied with secondary matters, it is easy to mistake the finish line. That was precisely David's sad failure toward the end of his life.

Wouldn't it have been wonderful if Psalm 18 was the closing prayer of David's life? Wouldn't it have been fitting? Well staged? Wouldn't it have made the perfect ending to the story? Perfect endings are hard to find in real life.

Perhaps David thought he saw the finish line. Maybe he subconsciously began to coast *to* the finish line instead of running *through* it. The character and ethos of the prayers of Psalm 18 and Psalm 30 clearly tell us something has transpired between the two, something exceedingly sad. Perhaps David began to think about his legacy. Maybe he started measuring what it had all meant, asking "How will history remember me?" or "Exactly how good am I?"

There is great debate about what exactly moved David to count his troops. God moved him (2 Sam. 24:1); Satan moved him (1 Chron. 21:1). Huh? Thus the debate.[2] What is clear is that neither God nor Satan forced David, he made up his own mind, presumably out of pride, to see just how powerful he really was—and it was wrong, dreadfully wrong. So wrong that even Joab's battle-hardened conscience recoiled at the thought (2 Sam. 24:3, 1 Chron. 21:3).

Joab and his men counted heads for almost ten months. Perhaps it was his own conscience or maybe other factors, but the census was not complete (1 Chron. 27:23–24), yet presumably close enough to feed the ego of the king who decided to coast to the finish line. But when the numbers were reported,[3] David immediately felt the conviction of God in his gut (2 Sam. 24:10). The prophet Gad announced the verdict. David chose the righteous mercy of God over the ruthless monarchs of the nations (2 Sam. 24:14, 1 Chron. 21:13).

The plague came, killing 70,000 of David's legacy (2 Sam. 24:15). When the angel of death reached the threshing floor of Araunah, the Lord stayed his hand. David beheld the angel with his drawn sword and purchased Araunah's property. He erected an altar there and worshiped the Lord. When Araunah offered the king the property and implements free of charge, David replied, "I will not offer burnt offerings to the LORD my God that cost me nothing" (2 Sam. 24:24). The fifty shekels of silver only began to tell the story of what it cost David to pray through the finish line—70,000 lives, dishonor, personal guilt. This prayer would cost him dearly.

Mercifully God gave David the vision of building a permanent dwelling place for God's presence in Jerusalem, and it was to be erected on Araunah's threshing floor. Though David would not be allowed to be its builder because of the blood on his hands, he would champion its cause, providing vast amounts of wealth and materials as well as organizing the leadership so that his son could build the temple. As David drew near the end of his life—having caught sight again of the finish line—he dedicated all this to the Lord for the building of his temple.

The final historically-footnoted psalm of David arose out of this failure and grace as he prepared to close out his life. This prayer powerfully reminds us of the necessity of praying through the finish line. It's always too soon to coast.

Ask yourself, what really matters in the end? After I have crossed the finish line, what will I look back upon as most significant in the race? A series of contrasts from David's closing prayer help us answer the questions. Praying through the finish line enables us to enjoy the difference between being lifted up rather than overcome (v. 1), songs of praise rather than cries of despair (vv. 1–2), health rather than sickness (v. 3), life rather than death (v. 3), blessing rather than discipline (vv. 5, 7), God's favor rather than God's anger (v. 5), the eternal rather than the momentary (v. 5), joy rather than sorrow (vv. 5, 11), God-reliance rather than self-reliance (v. 6), an audience with God rather than distance from Him (v. 7), stability rather than insecurity (v. 7) and living on to praise the Lord rather than the silence of death (vv. 8–9, 12).

As we prepare to close this study David reminds us that it is always too soon to look back and coast. Keep praying through! Why so urgent? David's final prayer tells us.

Psalm 30

A Psalm of David. A song at the dedication of the temple.

¹ I will extol you, O LORD, *for you have drawn me up*
and have not let my foes rejoice over me.
² O LORD *my God, I cried to you for help,*
and you have healed me.
³ O LORD, *you have brought up my soul from Sheol;*
you restored me to life from among those who go down to
the pit.

A Hand Reaching

You must keep praying because there is a hand reaching to you. Notice how David viewed what God had just done for him. Remember, God had judged him and the nation severely. Seventy-thousand people lost their lives because of David's pride. "I will extol you, O LORD, for you have *drawn me up* . . . O LORD, you have *brought up* my soul from Sheol; you restored me to life from among those who

> *No matter what you've done or what you are facing, keep praying because God is extending His hand of grace to you.*

go down to the pit" (vv. 1, 3). The verb is one used elsewhere to describe the pulling of a bucket up from the bottom of a well (Prov. 20:5). The imagery is of God in His exaltation reaching down to draw you up from the pit of your problem. The lingering image in David's mind was not an angel with a sword drawn in judgment, but God in His glory extending His hand in grace.

No matter what you've done or what you are facing,

keep praying because God is extending His hand of grace to you. He is reaching to you right where you are in the middle of your mess.

Remember how later Daniel would receive an unsettling vision from God, and would pray and mourn and fast for three weeks over it? Eventually an angel appeared to Daniel and said, "Fear not, Daniel, for from the first day that you set your heart to understand and humbled yourself before your God, your words have been heard, and I have come because of your words" (Dan. 10:12). From the moment you lift your voice to God, He begins extending His hand to you.

David said God "healed" him (v. 2). There is no mention of David actually becoming sick during the plague; yet surely he saw the destroying angel as coming down upon him as well, for he caused the plague. He believed he was to be numbered "among those who go down to the pit" (v. 3). It had been only the extension of God's gracious hand that delivered David. This, he was convinced, happened because he "cried to [God] for help" (v. 2).

Don't stop. Don't give in. Keep praying no matter how dark things appear. Pray *through* . . . because there is a hand reaching to you.

When I was a small child, my parents sent me to swimming lessons. I was deathly afraid of any water over about chest deep. As we neared the end of our series of lessons, the instructor told us we would be allowed to go in "the deep end" on our final day. The day arrived, the hour ran its course; and toward the end of the last lesson, we were led single-file to the far end of the pool—a land no small child felt ready for. The instructor gave careful instructions: One at a time we were to stand on the edge of the pool, at his signal we were to step off the side feet first into the water, descend to the bottom, push off the bottom and float back to the surface. Easy. Yeah, right! Through the shimmering surface of the water, I could see the eery sign at the bottom of the pool that said "13 feet." A lump formed in my throat.

One by one we took our turns. Finally I was next in line. The instructor rehearsed the instructions. I nodded my head, stepped out and was gone. My descent was easy (it always is!). When I reached the bottom I paused and asked myself a poorly timed question: "What was the step after 'touch the bottom'?" For a moment I thought, then, as my lungs began to burn, I panicked—*what next?!* I remembered a ladder had been about two feet to my left as I jumped in. I groped along the wall hopelessly, not realizing the ladder only extended a few feet below the surface of the water. Some time must have passed and with it any hope that I would recall the next step in the instructions. Panic is a strange thing, and it plays strange tricks on the mind.

Nearly beside myself by now, I suddenly felt a strong hand seize mine and jerk me to the surface. I drew a wild, frantic breath of air. My eyes met those of my instructor, who was now in the pool next to me. "What were you doing down there?" he inquired. I had no answer. There was no good answer. Though thoroughly embarrassed (and equally convinced I'd never enter "the deep end" again), I was profoundly thankful for a strong hand reaching out to me.

We must pray through the finish line, because praying

through is the means of moving from our strength to God's strength. It is always too soon to stop praying, because God's hand is reaching to you.

A Day Dawning

You must keep praying, because there is a new day dawning for you. Listen as David prays on:

> *⁴ Sing praises to the LORD, O you his saints,*
>   *and give thanks to his holy name.*
> *⁵ For his anger is but for a moment,*
>   *and his favor is for a lifetime.*
> *Weeping may tarry for the night,*
>   *but joy comes with the morning.*

These are probably the best known words of this entire psalm, and for good reason: We often feel lost in the darkness.

Aron Ralston was an experienced outdoorsman on a carefree desert hike. He had selected Blue John Canyon in Southeastern Utah for a solo trek that was to last a couple of days. When at the bottom of a narrow passageway an 800-pound bolder rolled over on his lower arm, he was plunged into a fight for his life. He was 100 feet below the surface of the desert and twenty miles from a paved road. He was surrounded by countless miles of desert wilderness—and he was alone. After five days in his pit of despair, Aron lost all hope. In desperation he attempted the unthinkable. Unable to dislodge his arm, he finally took his pocketknife and severed his arm from his body. Starving, severely dehydrated, bleeding profusely and battling shock, Aron managed a sixty-five foot rappel down a rock face and then began his hike to hope. Having survived the ordeal of a lifetime, he was asked what was the most difficult part of the horrifying ordeal. The answer, said Aron, was simple: the nights, the cold, utter blackness of the nights.

Who of us, even though we've thankfully never endured what Aron has, can't understand that feeling?

Having emerged from the long night of judgment, David testified, "Weeping may tarry for the night" (v. 5). The word translated "tarry" more literally means something like "will spend the night" or "lodges." Weeping is personified as a stranger who has come to your home seeking shelter. Having opened your door, you endure a long night of sobs sounding out of the darkness. Your only hope is that the dawn of a new day will drive the tears away.

> *Our earthly sorrows are brief compared to the joy that will follow. This is the great hope of God's people throughout the ages, in every imaginable darkness.*

The promise is, of course, not a guarantee of a specific time frame (all problems resolved in twelve hours or less!). It declares instead that our sorrows are brief compared to the joy that will follow. Hasn't this been the great hope of God's people throughout the ages and in every imaginable darkness?

This I call to mind, and therefore I have hope: The steadfast love of the LORD never ceases; his mercies never come to an end; they are new every morning; great is your faithfulness. (Lam. 3:21-23)

When a woman is giving birth, she has sorrow because
her hour has come, but when she has delivered the baby,
she no longer remembers the anguish, for joy that a human being has been born into the world. (John 16:21)

I consider that the sufferings of this present time are
not worth comparing with the glory that is to be revealed
to us. (Rom. 8:18)

The first of these chronologically-considered psalms set
forth this same lesson. When Saul sent his men to watch
over David's house by night and capture and kill him, David
had prayed, "Each evening they come back, howling like
dogs and prowling about the city. . . . But I will sing of
your strength; I will sing aloud of your steadfast love in
the morning" (Ps. 59:14, 16). David ended on the same
note with which he'd begun. His hope endured, and it
paid off. From beginning to end we must resolve to pray
through, because it is the means of moving from darkness
to light.

A Heart Forming

You must keep praying because there is a heart forming in you. David confessed,

> ⁶ *As for me, I said in my prosperity,*
> *"I shall never be moved."*

The word "prosperity" describes a careless ease, a presumption that things will continue in their present pattern
with no interruption to one's pleasures. Hadn't this been

the heart-problem that provoked David to take the census of his military? David's assertion, "I will never be moved," was borrowed from the arrogantly wicked (Ps. 10:6). Sadly, the man after God's own heart now soiled it with his own evil pride.

"Where is the hope in this?" you might ask.

> *7 By your favor, O LORD,*
> *you made my mountain stand strong;*
> *you hid your face;*
> *I was dismayed.*

David's "mountain" refers to Mount Zion, which was the center of David's kingdom. God had promised that Jerusalem would be led by a dynasty of rulers from David's descendants. The promise, despite the discipline, still stood. "You hid your face; I was dismayed." But when God smiles upon us, we stand. When He looks away, we dissolve.

It reminds me of recent days at my son's soccer game. At the introductory level at which he is currently playing, every child kicks the ball and looks to the sidelines. There is a connection between the foot and the head: The foot swings, the head turns, looking for a sign of approval from mom or dad on the sidelines. We never quite graduate out of that need for God's countenance to smile upon us in grace.

Keep praying, because praying through is the means of moving from self-reliance to God-reliance.

A Purpose Seizing

You must keep praying because there is a purpose seizing on you. Dead men write no psalms! Dead men sing no songs! This was David's reasoning as he continued in prayer:

> [8] *To you, O LORD, I cry,*
>   *and to the LORD I plead for mercy:*
> [9] *"What profit is there in my death,*
>   *if I go down to the pit?*
> *Will the dust praise you?*
>   *Will it tell of your faithfulness?"*

⌐⌐

The ultimate purpose of life is to be a worshiper. Through the mess of life we lose track of it. Praying through is the means of moving from self-absorption to worship.

David did not attempt to argue God into a corner or to twist His arm into sparing his life. Rather in prayer he held up to God the purpose of his life, and all of our lives. That purpose is to be a worshiper of God. It is why we were redeemed. It is why we remain. A.W. Tozer explains:

Why did Christ come? Why was He conceived? Why was He born? Why was He crucified? Why did He rise again? Why is He now at the right hand of the Father?

The answer to all these questions is, "In order that He might make worshipers out of rebels; in order that He might restore us again to the place of worship we knew when we were first created."[4]

Think of it—70,000 people had died. Don't soft-sell that. Don't water it down. That's a lot of corpses. That's a mess! That's a lot of wailing, crying and despair. And it was David's fault. Why should he live? What reason could he give? Was it, "God, where are you going to find a better songwriter than me?" Hardly!

David had long been a composer of worship songs. Before he'd even appeared on the stage of Israel's leadership, he was designated "a man after [God's] own heart" (1 Sam. 13:14). Though through the mess of life he'd lost track of it, he was now coming back to the purpose of his life.

> *10 "Hear, O LORD, and be merciful to me!*
> *O LORD, be my helper!"*

You must keep praying because praying through is the means of moving from self-absorption to worship.

A Joy Bubbling Up

You must keep praying because there is a joy bubbling up in you. David closed this final prayer this way:

> *11 You have turned for me my mourning into dancing;*
> *you have loosed my sackcloth*
> *and clothed me with gladness,*
> *12 that my glory may sing your praise and not be silent.*
> *O LORD my God, I will give thanks to you forever!*

If you will press through the present distress in prayer, you will find at some point along the path a fresh infusion of heaven-sent joy bubbling up from within you. Do you hear the transformation that has taken place in the process of praying through? David has gone from wailing to dancing, from graveclothes to joy!

What creates joy? Only one thing—the hand of God moving on your behalf: "you have drawn me up . . . healed me . . . brought up my soul . . . restored me to life . . . made my mountain strong . . . turned . . . my wailing into dancing . . . loosed my sackcloth and clothed me with gladness"!

This sackcloth was more than metaphor and poetic expression, for David and the other leaders of Israel had donned sackcloth to demonstrate their repentance before God (1 Chron. 21:16). Can you imagine the horror of watching people drop like flies around you? Can you imagine the joy that must have erupted when the destroying angel stayed his hand? David described it as "my glory may sing to your praise and not be silent" (v. 12).

I've heard many different voices sing—some good and some, well, you know. I've heard recording artists and shower-singers. I've heard sopranos, altos, tenors and bases. But I have to ask myself: When was the last time I heard someone's "glory" sing? What exactly does that sound like? It must include a lot more than just a pleasing voice, for it refers to the whole of one's being. Singing with my "glory" means that everything in me at my best and brightest is put into an expression of joy over God's goodness and grace. Anyone, no matter the quality of their voice, can sing with their "glory," and when they finally do, they'll "not be silent."

It was his "glory" which David had been trying to measure when the whole fiasco of the census started. Now he's seen God's glory, and he understands the place of his own glory in the grand scheme of things. The candle thinks it's a big deal in the pitch of a moonless night, but let the sun rise and it realizes just how outclassed it is. True joy comes from gathering up your very best and devoting it, not to your own glory, but to God's.

Keep praying, because there is a hand reaching out to you, a day dawning upon you, a heart forming within you, a purpose seizing hold of you and a joy about to bubble up within you. Keep praying, because it is the means of moving from your strength into God's, from darkness to light, from self-reliance to God-reliance, from self-absorption to worship and from despair to joy.

On October 29, 1941, while Europe was becoming bitterly embroiled in a life-defining conflict, Winston Churchill visited his alma mater, Harrow School. At the invitation of the headmaster, he addressed the boys. Looking back over the ten months that had passed since he'd last visited them, Churchill delivered what have become immortal words of hope:

> Surely from this period of ten months this is the lesson: never give in, never give in, never, never, never, never . . . never yield to the apparently overwhelming might of the enemy. We stood all alone a year ago, and to many countries it seemed that our account was closed, we were finished. All this tradition of ours, our sons, our School history, this part of the history of this country, were gone and liquidated.
>
> Very different is the mood today.

In practical terms, praying through is our stubborn refusal to give up. Praying through is how we run *through* the finish line. Indeed, "You have need of endurance, so that when you have done the will of God you may receive what is promised" (Heb. 10:36).

We began this journey by asserting that these psalms of David, chronologically considered, would enable us to pray through the problems of life. By now we have prayed through betrayal, vulnerability, humiliation, loneliness, atrocity, treachery, self-vindication, reality, guilt, personal disaster, slander and through a lifetime of both joys and struggles. These, of course, are only the beginning of the prayers we find in the psalter. Take these up again, as often as needed. Lay hold of the 136 others and make them yours; for as you do, you will keep praying through. Stay that course, and you will discover yourself emerging into the life God offers you.

Praying Through

As you rise from the pages of this book, open the Scriptures and pray through Psalm 30. You are right to close this book, but don't ever close the cover on the psalms, for when you do you are closing the books on your future.

- In prayer reach out and take the hand of grace God is extending to you. Ask Him to show you how to move from living in your own strength to living in His.

- Tell God how dark things seem right now. Admit to Him how uncertain you are about the future. Thank Him that he has brighter days ahead for you.

- Ask God to forgive you for resting in your comforts and pleasures. Confess how satisfied you've become with lesser things. Admit the precarious nature of depending on your own strength. Tell Him you are transferring your trust from circumstances and self to Him alone.

- Take up God's purpose for you: to become a worshiper. Move your eyes off of yourself and your circumstances and on to God. Commit to making praise a dominant part of your prayer life.

- Review your life and give thanks for the many evidences of God's work for your good. Consciously trade your depression and discouragement for hope. Sing a song of hope and praise to God. Thank Him in advance for moving you from despair to hope.

Epilogue

A LONE, bare light bulb. Plain, unadorned concrete walls and floor. A cement cot. A pot for one's waste. Life for a dissident Jew in the former Soviet Union was often a barren experience—but especially so for one in the Lefortovo or Chistopol prisons. But even this was "home" compared to the punishment cell used for disciplinary purposes. Anatoly spent plenty of time in both during his nine years of incarceration.

His crime? He cared about human rights enough to speak up. His greatest offense? He wanted to emigrate from the land of his birth (the Soviet Union) to the land of his people (Israel).

Anatoly had not been a particularly religious Jew. He had known and cared little for the history of his people. He did not know the God of his fathers. What he did begin to see was that life under the Soviet regime was not what it should be, or could be. And he set himself on a crusade to find that life.

During his nine years of imprisonment, Anatoly Sharansky spent 403 days in punishment cells and more than two hundred on hunger strikes. Months on end of countless, repeated interrogations, and then the contrasting stretches of extreme isolation, took their toll on body, mind and spirit. The experience of a punishment cell began with the humiliation of a strip search. With thin, worn clothing offered to replace the warmer clothing that had been confiscated, the offender was led to the basement where a bare cement room measuring two meters by one and a half awaited him. The walls were damp, the plaster flaked and peeled from the moisture. There was no cot, only a cement stump in the center that was nearly too small to sit on. A lone lightbulb located above the door broke the darkness and allowed the guards to observe the "guest" through the peephole. At bedtime the door would swing open, and a guard would unlock a large wooden plank that swung down from the wall. Here, without mattress or blankets, one fought to wrestle sleep from the clutches of the night. For some it was the hunger induced by scanty provisions. For others the boredom is what consumed them. For Anatoly it was the cold; the pervasive, inescapable chill was his worst enemy.

His ordeal began on March 15, 1977, when the KGB abducted him on Gorky Street. He was snatched from his new bride, his family, his life, his home. He was thrust into a desperate struggle for physical survival and into a desperate search for real life. It was over two and a half years into his struggle that Anatoly unexpectedly received a ray of light and hope. On January 21, 1980—the day after his 32nd birthday—an official who was in charge of storing prisoners' belongings inexplicably brought to him a small black book that had been confiscated from his apartment when the KGB had raided it at the time of his arrest. It had been a gift from his bride, Avital, who had emigrated to Israel just after their wedding in the anticipation that Anatoly would be permitted to follow soon. From Israel she had sent to him this little book of Psalms. Anatoly had tried since his incarceration to obtain the book from the storeroom, but had been denied. Now, without explanation, here it was—in his hands! To that point the book had been little more to Anatoly than a sentimental gift from his wife. When he held it, he in some respect felt he held her. It was precious to him. It connected him to Avital.

The following evening the food trap in the door of his cell flung open and a telegram was thrust through the opening. With shaking hands Anatoly read the lines, "My dearest son! Yesterday, on January 20, Papa passed away. Please bear this sorrow as bravely as I did. Natasha and I are well, and are with you all the time. I kiss you affectionately. Mama."[1]

Anatoly was plunged into a darkness that not even this prison had been able to send over him. For two days he sat in benumbed shock, not wanting to move, think or do anything. Then the thought of his Psalm book came to him. Suddenly an overwhelming urge to read it swept over him. "I opened it," Anatoly recollected, "and immediately decided that I must read all 150 of the Psalms—not sometime in the future, but starting today."

The print was small. The light was bad. His eyes burned from the strain. He didn't recognize some of the Hebrew words; but by working from roots that he knew and guessing at others, he was able, slowly and meticulously to begin, to digest each line. As he first took hold of what would become his lifeline over the coming seven years, Anatoly admitted, "I can't say that I understood the Psalms completely, but I sensed their spirit and felt both the joy and the suffering of King David, their author."[2] He recalled as a child having seen an awe-inspiring statue of a man, whose foot rested on a huge head. Later his father explained to him the account of David and Goliath—his first lesson in things Jewish. As he began to immerse himself in the Psalms, the distant memory flooded back into his conscious thoughts. Later he would reflect, "And now, in my cell, King David had come to my aid."[3]

In time the prison guards, officials and interrogators took note of Anatoly's attachment to that tiny black book. Before long it became their leverage point with him. Eventually, in the dead of the Russian winter, they confiscated his book of Psalms. His objections were met with the dry party line he had come to expect: "It is the duty of the state to guard you in prison from harmful influence, so your religious literature has been confiscated with our consent."[4]

Nothing could have struck him more deeply. It had become increasingly difficult to distinguish the line of demarcation between the words of the Psalms and the life of Anatoly Sharansky. Life without the Psalms was unthinkable, impossible; it would be . . . not life at all.

Anatoly declared a work strike until they returned his book of Psalms. The Soviet officials responded in kind, denying Anatoly any visits from family for the next two years. When he didn't budge, they sentenced him to fifteen days in the punishment cell. Over two weeks later they asked, "Are you going to work?" His reply was simple,

"Only when you return my Psalm book." He was given fifteen more days in the punishment cell.

The standoff continued until Anatoly had spent seventy-five days in the punishment cell. By now he was nearly overcome with weakness. But when asked again if he would return to work, he replied as he had so many times before, "Only when you return by Psalm book." The resolve of the prison officials wavered only slightly, "Five days in the punishment cell."

The battle went on—repeated demands to return to work, each met with Anatoly's refusal until the Psalms were returned. By the time he neared his one-hundredth day in the prison cell, Anatoly's weakness was becoming overwhelming. Once as he tried to stand, everything turned dark, his head filled with a deafening roar and then—blackness. He was transferred to the prison hospital. There he regained some strength, but soon he was back in the punishment cell.

Again, "Will you go to work?" Again, "Not until you give me back my Psalm book." Another fifteen days. On and on the test of wills continued. Eventually the Soviets transferred Anatoly to another prison. Shortly after his arrival they brought him materials for weaving bags that were used to carry vegetables and demanded, "Start working."

"What about my Psalm book?"

Amazingly, it was only a few days until Anatoly held in his hand the small book of Psalms.[5] In all he had spent 186 days in the punishment cell, but in the end he deemed it worth the privilege of latching hold again of the words that had become his words, the lines that had become his life.[6]

The coming years of his nearly one-decade stay in Soviet prisons unfolded day by day. Every day was spent with
the Psalms giving voice to his soul's deepest cries. Then on
the morning of February 10, 1986, the food trap in the
door of his cell slammed open and a gruff voice ordered,
"To a summons."

Guards undressed Anatoly. Everything he possessed was
confiscated. He was given different clothing—civilian clothing. He asked for a belt, for the pants he'd been given were
far too large. He was given a piece of string. Without explanations he was led to the exit of the prison where four
KGB men awaited him. Not knowing what awaited him,
Anatoly demanded, "I want my Psalm book with me."
They tried to forcibly remove him, but Anatoly began to
lift screams that echoed off the stark prison walls. Soon
one of the KGB officers produced the book and said,
"You'll receive it on the spot."

Outside the prison Anatoly was forced into a car as
photographers captured every move. In an escort of three
cars he was sped through the streets of Moscow. "Where
to this time?" Anatoly wondered to himself. His heart
soared with anticipation as it became increasingly clear
they were taking him to Bykovo airport. As they entered
the airport the car proceeded to a waiting plane. Before
the car doors could open, Anatoly saw another band of
photographers jostle for position.

So much confusion. So many questions. Where was he
headed? Could this really be it? Was he going to be released? Would they really send him to Israel to be reunited
with Avital after 12 years of married life spent virtually
entirely apart? Could he dare believe?

As he stepped out of the car and before moving toward the plane, he demanded one more time, "Where's my Psalm book?" "You received everything that was permitted," came the brusque reply. As the officers moved to take him away to the plane Anatoly dropped to the snow in protest. "I won't move until you give me back my Psalm book." No one moved. The photographers were poised to capture every move, every word of this now world-renown human rights activist.

Everything Anatoly had ever wanted lay just yards in front of him. Freedom. Israel. Avital. But seeing no movement in response to his demand, Anatoly lay back in the snow and screamed, "*Give me back my Psalm book!*"

Within moments the book was begrudgingly thrust into his hands. He was put upon the plane. Soon he was airborne, but still he did not know where he was headed. He could only hope, dream, pray. After two hours of flight time toward the setting sun, an official informed him that he was being deported from the Soviet Union, having been charged with espionage.

His day had finally come. "It was over." Anatoly dropped into his seat amazed. "I knew all along that this day would have to come," he would later write. "And now I took the Psalm book and turned to Psalm 30, which I had long ago decided to recite at the moment of my release. 'A song of David at the dedication of a house,' it began. Now I was reading these words en route to my own house in Jerusalem! . . . I continued reading one triumphant psalm after another."[7]

Within days Anatoly stood physically in Jerusalem—finally reunited with Avital, having obtained his dream, having won. Anatoly made his way through a crush of people to the western wall of the Old City. "Holding our Psalm book in my hand, I kissed the wall and said, '*Baruch matir asirim.*' Blessed is He who liberates the imprisoned."[8]

· · · · ·

"He who liberates the imprisoned." He lives today. He is still in the liberation business. He is the One David pursued in prayer. He lives, having emerged triumphant from death and leaving behind an empty tomb. He is the One bidding you to pray through. He is the Life ready to embrace you. May you pray through until you can genuinely cry, "Blessed is He who liberates the imprisoned!"

Appendix

The Reliability of Psalm Titles

Scholars from the critical school of thought have long debunked the genuineness and reliability of the psalm titles. J.W. Thirtle in his groundbreaking article "The Titles of the Psalms" (1905) demonstrated that some elements of the psalm titles (such as musical directions) may have been originally intended as a postscript to the previous psalm, rather than a superscription to the psalm to which it is assigned in most of our Bibles. Thirtle, however, has demonstrated sufficiently that the historical footnotes give every evidence of being genuine and intended as prescripts to the psalms before which they appear in most of our English translations.

The psalm titles originated at an early date when more exact information about their original composition would likely have been in possession of those affixing the titles. Some designate the psalm titles as a part of the canonical text in the Hebrew Bible (e.g., Boice, James Montgomery, *Psalms*, Grand Rapids, Michigan: Baker Book House, 1994;

1:29) and demand that they should be treated with the respect we give the other parts of that text. Other conservative scholars, while accepting the historical reliability of the titles, do not assign them to the canonical text. There is also debate as to whether the Hebrew *lamed* ("*of* David") means "belonging to" or "concerning." Either translation is possible.

We do well to realize that Jesus also took these titles as historically accurate and reliable (cf. Ps. 110:1 and Matt. 22:43–45; Mark 12:35–37; Lk. 20:41–44), as did Peter and Luke (Ps. 41:9 and Acts 1:16; Jn. 13:18; Ps. 16:8–11 and Acts 2:25–28; Ps. 110:1 and Acts 2:34–35) and Paul (Ps. 32:1–2 and Rom. 4:6; Ps. 69:22–23 and Rom. 11:9–10).

Many current Biblical scholars affirm the reliability of the psalm titles, such as: Gleason L. Archer (*A Survey of Old Testament Introduction: Revised and Expanded*, Chicago: Moody Press, 1964, 1974, 1994, pp.496, 497), Hassell C. Bullock (*An Introduction to the Old Testament Poetic Books: Revised and Expanded*, Chicago: Moody Press, 1979, 1988, p.122), Derek Kidner (*Psalm 1-72: An Introduction and Commentary*, Downers Grove, Illinois: Inter-Varsity Press, 1973, pp. 32–33), and Allen P. Ross ("Psalms" in *The Bible Knowledge Commentary*, Victor Books, 1988, vol. 1, p.782.

Spurgeon seems to have found the better part of wisdom when he comments on the title to Psalm 59: "Great efforts were made to carry the Psalms away to other authors and seasons than those assigned in the headings. . . . We are not anxious to show our readiness for conjecture, and therefore are content with reading this Psalm in the light of the circumstances here mentioned; it does not seem unsuitable to any verse, and in some the words are very appropriate to the specified occasion" (Spurgeon, C.H., *The Treasury of David: An Expository and Devotional Commentary on the Psalms*, Fincastle, Virginia: Scripture Truth Book Co., reprint 1984, 1:1043).

Endnotes

Prologue

1. Norris, Kathleen, "Why the Psalms Scare Us," *Christianity Today*, July 15, 1996, p.19.

2. Quoted in Norris, p.20.

3. See Appendix: The Reliability of Psalm Titles, p. 255.

4. The general chronology of these fourteen psalms appears clear. The exact identification of a few, however, remains a challenge. For example, Psalm 7 bears the superscription "of David, which he sang to the Lord concerning Cush, a Benjamite." There is no mention of a "Cush" from the tribe of Benjamin in the historical records of First and Second Samuel. Yet, as is explained in chapter 12, there is good reason for placing it where we have. Similarly, the chronology behind the note "For the dedication of the temple" attached to Psalm 30 is up for debate. Yet, again, good reasons move us to place it at the last of these psalms. To which of David's cave-experiences do we assign Psalms 57 and 142? Do they belong to Adullam or Engedi? Which came first? In these cases, the understanding is not so much tied to a strict chronology as it is to the general historical context that clearly

stands behind these superscriptions and the psalms to which they are attached.

Chapter 1: Praying Through Betrayal

1. Read First Samuel 19:8–12 for the historical background to Psalm 59. The dramatized accounts that begin each chapter admittedly extend beyond the bare facts given us in the historical accounts of First and Second Samuel. Be certain not to confuse the two. However, these dramatizations are provided to help us identify more fully with the circumstances from which and the emotion with which each psalm was composed.

2. For other expressions of this concern see Psalm 7:6; 35:23; 44:23; 78:65.

3. Kidner, Derek, *Psalms 1–72: An Introduction and Commentary on Books I and II of the Psalms* (Downers Grove, IL: InterVarsity, 1973), 212–213.

4. VanGemeren, Willem A., "Psalms" in *The Expositor's Bible Commentary* (Grand Rapids, MI: Zondervan, 1991), 5:411.

5. "Three different words are used for this, which might be rendered 'I will sing . . . I will shout . . . (16); I will raise a psalm' (17)." (Kidner, 214)

6. Boice, James Montgomery, *Psalms: An Expositional Commentary* (Grand Rapids, MI: Baker Books, 1996), 2:493.

Chapter 2: Praying Through Vulnerability

1. Read First Samuel 21:10–12 for the historical background to Psalm 56.

2. Alexander, Joseph Addison , *The Psalms: Translated and Expanded* (Grand Rapids, MI: Zondervan, reprint, n.d.), 249.

3. White, William, "rā'â," *Theological Wordbook of the Old Testament* (Chicago: Moody, 1980), 2:824.

4. Maclaren, Alexander, *The Life of David as Reflected in His Psalms* (Grand Rapids, MI: Baker, 1955), 79.

5. This is the ESV's marginal reading, in place of "they injure my cause."

6. Kidner, Derek, *Psalms 1–72: An Introduction and Commentary on Books I and II of the Psalms* (Downers Grove, IL: Inter-Varsity Press, 1973), 203.

7. Boice, James Montgomery, *Psalms: An Expositional Commentary* (Grand Rapids, MI: Baker Books, 1996), 2:471.

8. "For no good reason, RSV alters the Hebrew text from 'wanderings' to *tossings*. No doubt both were true, but 'wandering' was David's special lot . . ." (Kidner, 204).

9. He is not alone in these weary flights from Gibeah to Ramah, from Ramah to Nob, from Nob to Gath, from Gath to he knows not whither. One friend goes with him through them all." (Maclaren, 81)

10. Leupold, H.C., *Exposition of the Psalms* (Grand Rapids, MI: Baker, 1969), 430.

Chapter 3: Praying Through Humiliation

1. Read 1 Samuel 21:10–22:2 for the historical background of Psalm 34.

2. Some debate why the king is here called Abimelech rather

than Achish, as in 1 Samuel. It is likely that Abimelech was a dynastic title among the Philistines, much like Pharaoh was among the Egyptians. Achish was probably the king's given name.

3. That this prayer arose from deep contemplation of God's grace is signaled by the fact that it is an acrostic. Each verse begins with the successive letter of the Hebrew alphabet, except for *waw*, between verses 5 and 6. This leaves the final verse standing outside the pattern (perhaps for special emphasis on God's ability to redeem us even from our lowest moments). Was the slightly "imperfect" acrostic form an intentional device, employed to match the less than ideal nature of the circumstances from which it arose? Such an orderly arrangement arising from such chaotic events and emotions is a signal that David did not run from his humiliation, but prayed through to a place of resolution.

4. e.g. Boice, James Montgomery, *Psalms: An Expositional Commentary* (Grand Rapids, MI: Baker Books, 1994), 2:296; Phillips, John, *Exploring the Psalms* (Neptune, NJ: Loizeaux Brothers, 1988), 1:259; Wiersbe, Warren W., *The Bible Exposition Commentary: Wisdom and Poetry* (Colorado Springs: Victor, 2004), 159.

5. Bryson, Bill, *A Short History of Nearly Everything* (New York: Broadway Books, 2003), 274.

6. The word translated "fears" in verse 4 is a stronger term than that employed (vv. 7, 9, 11) to describe the fear of the Lord. This word describes the terror of out-of-control circumstances, the latter the reverential awe of God.

Chapter 4: Praying Through Loneliness

1. Study 1 Samuel 22:1–2 for the background of Psalm 142. Since the psalm title points simply to a time when David "was

in the cave," it is possible that it may have arisen from the events of 1 Samuel 24:4 when David took refuge in the cave of Engedi. However, the contents of the psalm seem to point to a time when David was completely alone (v. 4), as in 1 Samuel 22:1–2, rather than surrounded by a small army of men, as in 1 Samuel 24:4. The tone here is more desperate and seems to match the events following his flight from Achish in Gath.

2. Taken from *Encouragement* by Dan B. Allender; Lawrence J. Crabb, Jr. copyright © 1984 by The Zondervan Corporation. Used by permission of Zondervan.

Chapter 5: Praying Through Atrocity

1. Read 1 Samuel 21:1–9 and 22:6–23 for the background to Psalm 52.

2. Boice, James Montgomery, *Psalms: An Expositional Commentary* (Grand Rapids, MI: Baker, 1996), 2:442.

3. Leupold, H.C., *Exposition of the Psalms* (Grand Rapids, MI: Baker, reprint 1969), 412.

4. Newsweek, June 21, 1993.

5. Boice, 2:443.

Chapter 6: Praying Through Treachery

1. Read 1 Samuel 23:1–26 for the background of Psalm 54.

2. Alternatively, many Hebrew manuscripts and the Targum have the Hebrew word *zēḏîm* ("proud"), instead of *zārîm* ("strangers"). Allan Harman, *Psalms* (Ross-shire: Christian Focus, 1998), 208.

3. Kaiser, Walter C., Jr., "Name," *The Zondervan Pictorial Encyclopedia of the Bible* (Grand Rapids, MI: Zondervan, 1975, 1976), 4:363.

4. Kaiser, Walter C., Jr., "sh m," *Theological Wordbook of the Old Testament* (Chicago: Moody, 1980), 2:934.

5. Thus the English "Jehovah" in some Bibles.

6. Leupold, H.C., *Exposition of the Psalms* (Grand Rapids, MI: Baker, 1969), 419.

7. "See the man who would not *make* God his refuge" (Ps. 52:7a).

8. Kidner, Derek, *Psalms 1–72: An Introduction and Commentary on Books I and II of the Psalms* (Downers Grove, IL: Inter-Varsity Press, 1973), 197.

9. Tozer, A.W., *The Knowledge of the Holy* (San Francisco: Harper Row, 1961), 1.

10. Willem A. VanGemeren ["Psalms," in *The Expositor's Bible Commentary* (Grand Rapids, MI: Zondervan, 1991), 5:389)] displays the structure of the psalm this way:
    A. Prayer for Deliverance (vv. 1–2)
        B. Occasion of the Prayer (v. 3)
            C. Affirmation of Trust (v. 4)
        B.' Resolution of the Prayer (v. 5)
    A.' Thanksgiving for the Deliverance (vv. 6–7)

11. Davis, Dale Ralph, *Looking on the Heart: Expositions of 1 Samuel (Volume 2—1 Samuel 15–31)* (Grand Rapids, MI: Baker, 1994), 98.

12. Cole, C. Donald, *Thirsting for God: A Devotional Study of the Psalms, in Light of their Historical Background* (Westchester, IL: Crossway, 1986), 151.

Chapter 7: Praying Through Vengeance

1. Read 1 Samuel 23:29–24:22 for the historical background of Psalm 57.

2. Reprinted with permission of *The Dallas Morning News.*

3. The psalm's title says only that it arose "when he fled from Saul, in the cave." Some have noted that does not definitely fix the occasion with that of First Samuel 23:29–24:22, saying it could well have arisen from David's stay in the Cave of Adullam (1 Sam. 22:1–2). As we have noted in chapter 4, Psalm 142 more naturally fits the situation in the Cave of Adullam. Likewise Psalm 57 better fits the circumstances around David's stay in the Cave of Engedi. Psalm 142 is more frantic, reflecting David's state of mind after fleeing Achish. Similarly Psalm 57 exudes a more restful calm that may have come from David's now protracted flight from Saul. The title here adds the notion that it arose out of Saul's pursuit of David. When he stayed in Adullam, David was fleeing Achish, not Saul. The fact that Psalm 57 is composed according to a tune entitled "Do Not Destroy" may be reflective of David's present refusal to destroy Saul (1 Sam. 24:4). The phrase "till the storms of destruction pass by" (Ps. 57:1) may also be re flective of the panic David and his men experienced as Saul entered the very cave they had made their refuge.

4. Note, for example, the title to Psalm 18.

5. cf. Ps. 7:2; 17:12; 22:13, 21; 34:10; 35:17; 58:6.

6. cf. Ps. 7:15–16; 9:15–16; 10:2; 35:7–8; 140:9; 141:10.

7. Wiseman, Donald J., "hāsâ," *Theological Wordbook of the Old Testament* (Chicago: Moody, 1980), 1:307–308.

8. cf. Ps. 17:8; 36:7; 61:4; 63:7.

9. Oswalt, John N., "kûn," *Theological Wordbook of the Old Testament* (Chicago: Moody, 1980), 1:433–434.

Chapter 8: Praying Through Reality

1. Read 2 Samuel 8 and 1 Chronicles 18 for the background to Psalm 60.

2. Leupold, H.C., *Exposition of The Psalms* (Grand Rapids, MI: Baker, 1969), 449.

3. According to the NIV's rendering.

Chapter 9: Praying Through Guilt

1. See 2 Samuel 11:1–12:23 for the background of Psalm 51.

2. Larsen, David, "The Transformation of a Terrorist," *The Voice From the Cross*, ed. Richard Allen Bodey (Grand Rapids, MI: Baker, 1990), 33.

3. Leupold, H.C., *Exposition of the Psalms* (Grand Rapids, MI: Baker, reprint 1969), 404.

4. Chambers, Oswald, *My Utmost For His Highest* (New York: Dodd, Mead Company, 1935, 1963), 160.

5. Colson, Charles, quoted in Edythe Draper, *Draper's Book of Quotations for the Christian World* (Wheaton, IL: Tyndale, 1992), 529.

6. Do not merely say, "I'm sorry." Humble yourself and say, "I sinned against you when I _____. I am very sorry. Would you please forgive me?" Give them the grace of time to process the change in your heart. Do not hinge your continued obedience upon their response.

Chapter 10: Praying Through Personal Disaster

1. Read Second Samuel 15–17 for the historical background of Psalm 3.

2. "A Bible student who probes more deeply into the problems here involved may well recall that the position in which David finds himself may have called for at least some reference to his own guilt and sin. For it is unquestionable that, according to Second Sam. 12:10, the whole train of evil consequences that befell his house had been set in motion by his own sin in the matter of Bathsheba and Uriah, the Hittite." (Leupold, H.C., *Exposition of the Psalms,* Grand Rapids, MI: Baker, re print 1969, 59–60.)

3. Leupold, H.C., *Exposition of the Psalms* (Grand Rapids, MI: Baker, reprint 1969), 60.

4. Anderson, A.A., *The Book of Psalms: Volume I Psalms 1–72*, New Century Bible Commentary, Ronald E. Clements and Matthew Black, gen. eds. (Grand Rapids, MI: Eerdmans, reprint 1995), 73 and Leupold, 61.

5. Anderson, A.A., 73.

6. Norris, Kathleen, "Why the Psalms Scare Us," *Christianity Today,* July, 15 1996, 21.

7. Clarke, Arthur G., *Analytical Studies in the Psalms* (Grand Rapids, MI: Kregel, 1979), 35.

8. VanGemeren, Willem A., "Psalms" in *The Expositor's Bible Commentary* (Grand Rapids, MI: Zondervan, 1991), 5:78.

9. Harman, Allan, *Psalms: A Mentor Commentary* (Ross-shire: Christian Focus, 1998), 77.

10. Wiersbe, Warren W., *The Bible Exposition Commentary: Old Testament History* (Colorado Springs: Victor, 2003), 350.

Chapter 11: Praying Through Spiritual Drought

1. Read Second Samuel 15:13–17:29 for the background to Psalm 63. Note especially 15:23, 28; 16:2, 15; 17:16.

2. Associated Press, "Marine's 'death march' investigated," Sheboygan Press, 19 December 1988, 8.

3. Tozer, A.W., *The Pursuit of God* (Camp Hill, Pennsylvania: Christian Publications, 1982), 15–16.

Chapter 12: Praying Through Slander

1. The title of Psalm 7 does not make specific the identity of Cush nor the time of his slander. We do note, however, that he was a Benjamite. That is to say he was of the same tribe as Saul. It is possible that he operated during the time of Saul's persecution of David (1 Sam. 14–16). But the Scriptures make clear that the resentments of Saul's household continued for years and from time to time flamed into a blaze again. We take up this psalm at this juncture because of the apparent similarity between his actions and those of Shimei (2 Sam. 16:5–14), and of those at an even later time by Sheba (2 Sam. 20). Reading through these passages will aid you in under standing David's circumstances in Psalm 7.

2. Brown, Francis, S.R. Driver, and Charles A. Briggs, *A Hebrew and English Lexicon of the Old Testament With an Appendix Containing the Biblical Aramaic* (Oxford: Clarendon Press, n.d.), 993.

3. This is, as we've already taken note in Psalm 3:7, military terminology reminiscent of Numbers 10:35, 36 (cf. also 2 Chron. 6:41–42).

4. Phillips, John, *Exploring the Psalms* (Neptune, NJ: Loizeaux Brothers, 1988), 1:62.

5. Boice, James Montgomery, *Psalms: An Expositional Commentary* (Grand Rapids, MI: Baker Books, 1994), 1:65.

Chapter 13: Praying Through Yesterday

1. Psalm 18 is repeated in Second Samuel 22 with only minor variations. The psalm arose "on the day when the Lord delivered him from the hand of all his enemies, and from the hand of Saul" (2 Sam. 22:1). This could mean, of course, that the psalm arose from the time just after Saul's death and David's ascendancy to the throne. Yet the Biblical writer, under inspiration of the Holy Spirit, placed it in the flow of events that closed out David's life. Indeed, it comes immediately before "the last words of David" (2 Sam. 23:1). Coming late in David's life, the prayer, with picturesque language, rehearses a lifetime of deliverance by God.

2. Quoted in Wiersbe, Warren and David Wiersbe, *Ministering to the Mourning* (Chicago: Moody, 2006), 183.

3. "The common word for 'love' is too weak for him, and he bends to his use another, never elsewhere employed to express man's emotions toward God, the intensity of which is but feebly expressed by some such periphrasis as, 'From my heart do I love Thee.'" (Maclaren, Alexander, *The Life of David As Reflected in His Psalms*, Grand Rapids, MI: Baker, reprint 1955, 157).

4. The chiastic structure of the psalm suggests these five keys:
Praise to God my Rock! (vv. 1–3)
    God's deliverance of David [in divine terms] (vv. 4–19)
        Why God delivered David (vv. 20–29)
    God's deliverance of David [in Davidic terms] (vv. 30–45)
Praise to God my Rock! (vv. 46–50)

5. All told David used twelve different names or titles for God in this psalm and employed them some thirty-four times. Fifty-nine times David ascribed action to God. There had been times when David had called God's actions into question (Ps. 60:1–3). There had been times when David felt God inactive (Ps. 3:7; 7:6–11). David was the one who uttered the words which would become our Lord's own question to his Father while he hung on the cross: "My God, my God, why have you forsaken me?" (Ps. 22:1). Yet, in the final analysis, David was able to look back over an entire lifetime and see how continuously God had been active on his behalf.

6. Quoted in Dale Ralph David, *2 Samuel: Looking on the Heart* (Ross-shire: Christian Focus, 1999), 233.

7. Boice, James Montgomery, *Psalms: An Expositional Commentary* (Grand Rapids, MI: Baker Books, 1994), 1:156.

8. M'Caw, Leslie S. and J.A. Motyer, "Psalms" in *The New Bible Commentary: Revised*, D. Guthrie, ed. (Grand Rapids, MI: Eerdmans, 1970), 461.

Chapter 14: Praying Through the Finish Line

1. Read Second Samuel 24 and First Chronicles 21ff for the background to Psalm 30. The title designates this as "A song at the dedication of the temple." The word translated "temple" is more simply "house," thus some claim this was more likely written for the dedication of David's personal palace (2 Sam. 5:11). Others protest that this could not have been a prayer for the dedication of the temple since that honor fell to David's son Solomon. Thus they claim that this was an existing psalm of David edited and made appropriate for that later occasion. By way of answer, I would simply state that the temple had been originally David's vision after the tragedy of his census (1 Chron. 22:1; 28:2), he provided the wealth and material for its completion (1 Chron. 22:2–19; 28:11–29:5), organized

the manpower for its operations and the overall success of the nation under a new king (1 Chron. 23–27), and then he held a dedication ceremony offering to God his son, his wealth, and his vision for the temple (1 Chron. 29:10–19). David was looking forward to this crowning achievement with great faith, although he knew it would occur after his own death. Perhaps David authored this prayer as a part of this dedication service or in anticipation of the completed temple in future days.

2. For an excellent discussion of the issues see Dale Ralph Davis, *2 Samuel: Looking on the Heart* (Ross-shire: Christian Focus, 1999), 257–259.

3. For clarity on the discrepancy between the numbers of Second Samuel 24:9 and First Chronicles 21:5 refer to Ronald F. Youngblood, "1, 2 Samuel," *The Expositor's Bible Commentary* (Grand Rapids, MI: Zondervan, 1992), 3:1098–1099.

4. Tozer, A.W., *The Best of A.W. Tozer* (Camp Hill, PA: Christian Publications, 1978), compiled by Warren W. Wiersbe, 217.

Epilogue

1. Sharansky, Natan, *Fear No Evil: The Classic Memoir of One Man's Triumph Over a Police State* (New York: Public Affairs, 1988, 1998), 267. Reprinted by permission of PUBLICAFFAIRS, a member of Perseus Books Group.

2. Ibid., 269.

3. Ibid.

4. Ibid., 307.
5. Ibid., 318.

6. Ibid., 330.

7. Ibid., 401–405.

8. Ibid., 411.

Bibliography

Aharoni, Yohanan and Michael Avi-Yonah. *The MacMillian Bible Atlas: Revised Edition*. New York: MacMillian Publishing Company, 1977.

Alexander, Joseph Addison. *The Psalms Translated and Explained*. Grand Rapids, MI: Zondervan Publishing House, undated reprint of original 1864 edition.

Anderson, A.A. *Psalms (1–72)*. The New Century Bible Commentary. Grand Rapids, MI: William B. Eerdmans Publishing Company, reprint 1995.

Anderson, A.A. *Psalms (73–150)*. The New Century Bible Commentary. Grand Rapids, MI: William B. Eerdmans Publishing Company, reprint 1995.

Boice, James Montgomery. *Psalms: An Expositional Commentary*, 3 vols. Grand Rapids, MI: Baker Books, 1994, 1996, 1998.

Bratcher, Robert G. and William G. Reyburn. *A Handbook on Psalms*. New York: United Bible Societies, 1991.

Clarke, Arthur G. *Analytical Studies in the Psalms*. Grand Rapids, MI: Kregel Publications, 1979.

Cole, C. Donald. *Thirsting for God: A Devotional Study of the Psalms, in Light of their Historical Background*. Westchester, IL: Crossway Books, 1986.

Davis, Dale Ralph. *Looking on the Heart: Expositions of 1 Samuel 1–14*. Grand Rapids, MI: Baker Books, 1994.

Davis, Dale Ralph. *Looking on the Heart: Expositions of 1 Samuel 15–31*. Grand Rapids, MI: Baker Books, 1994.

Davis, Dale Ralph. *2 Samuel: Out of Every Adversity*. Ross-shire, UK: Christian Focus Publications, 1999.

Harman, Allan M. *Commentary on the Psalms*. Ross-shire, UK: Christian Focus Publications, 1998.

Henry, Matthew. *Matthew Henry's Commentary on the Whole Bible: Complete and Unabridged in One Volume*. Peabody, Massachusetts: Hendrikson Publishers, 1991.

Hibbard, F.G. *Commentary on the Old Testament: The Book of Psalms*. Salem, Ohio: Schmul Publishers, reprint 1979.

Kidner, Derek. *Psalms 1–72: An Introduction and Commentary on Books I and II of the Psalms.* Downers Grove, IL: InterVarsity Press, 1973.

Kidner, Derek. *Psalms 73–150: A Commentary on Books III–V of the Psalms.* Downers Grove, IL: InterVarsity Press, 1975.

Leupold, H.C. *Exposition of the Psalms.* Grand Rapids, MI: Baker Book House, reprint 1969.

Maclaren, Alexander. *The Life of David as Reflected in His Psalms.* Grand Rapids, MI: Baker Book House, reprint 1955.

M'Caw, Leslie S. and J.A. Motyer. "Psalms" in *The New Bible Commentary: Revised.* Grand Rapids, MI: William B. Eerdmans Publishing Company, 1970.

Nordstrom, Elaine. *A Chronological Arrangement of David's Psalms.* Master of Arts Thesis. Wheaton College, Wheaton, IL. 1951.

Phillips, John. *Exploring the Psalms Volume One: Psalms 1–88.* Neptune, NJ: Loizeaux Brothers, 1988.

Phillips, John. *Exploring the Psalms Volume Two: Psalms 89–150.* Neptune, NJ: Loizeaux Brothers, 1988.

Ross, Allen P. "Psalms" in *The Bible Knowledge Commentary*. Wheaton, IL: Victor Books, 1985.

Spurgeon, C.H. *The Treasury of David: An Expository and Devotional Commentary on the Psalms*. 2 vols. Fincastle, VA: Scripture Truth Book Company, reprint 1984.

VanGemeren, Willem A. "Psalms" in *The Expositor's Bible Commentary*, vol. 5. gen. ed., Frank E. Gaebelein. Grand Rapids, MI: Zondervan Publishing House, 1991.

Youngblood, Ronald F. "1, 2 Samuel" in *The Expositor's Bible Commentary*, vol.3. gen. ed., Frank E. Gaebelein. Grand Rapids, MI: Zondervan Publishing House, 1992.

Wiersbe, Warren W. *The Bible Exposition Commentary: History*. Colorado Springs, CO: Victor, 2003.

Wiersbe, Warren W. *The Bible Exposition Commentary: Wisdom and Poetry*. Colorado Springs, CO: Victor, 2004.

This book was produced by CLC Publications. We hope it has been life-changing and has given you a fresh experience of God through the work of the Holy Spirit. CLC Publications is an outreach of CLC Ministries International, a global literature mission with work in over 50 countries. If you would like to know more about us or are interested in opportunities to serve with a faith mission, we invite you to contact us at:

CLC Ministries International
PO Box 1449
Fort Washington, PA 19034

Phone: (215) 542-1242
E-mail: clcmail@clcusa.org
Website: www.clcusa.org

DO YOU LOVE GOOD CHRISTIAN BOOKS?
Do you have a heart for worldwide missions?

You can receive a FREE subscription to
CLC's newsletter on global literature missions
Order by e-mail at:

clcheartbeat@clcusa.org
or fill in the coupon below and mail to:

P.O. Box 1449
Fort Washington, PA 19034

FREE *HEARTBEAT* SUBSCRIPTION!
Name: _____
Address: _____
_____
Phone: _____ **E-mail:** _____

READ THE REMARKABLE STORY OF
the founding of
CLC International

"Any who doubt that Elijah's God still lives ought to read of the money supplied when needed, the stores and houses provided, and the appearance of personnel in answer to prayer."

—Moody Monthly

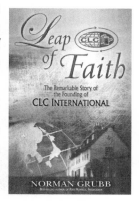

Is it possible that the printing press, the editor's desk, the Christian bookstore, and the mail order department, can glow with the fast-moving drama of an "Acts of the Apostles"?

Find out, as you are carried from two people in an upstairs bookroom to a worldwide chain of Christian bookcenters, multiplied by nothing but a "shoestring" of faith and committed, though unlikely, lives.

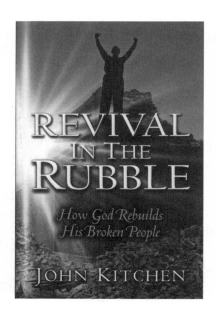

REVIVAL IN THE RUBBLE

JOHN KITCHEN

Rubble: the crumbled remains of a previous generation's true spiritual experience with God.

Can spiritual life and renewal ever be found in the midst of such devastation?

Yes, says John Kitchen. *"When God wants to do a fresh, reviving work in His people, He finds a person and breaks his heart."*

"You'll be delighted with this user-friendly approach to allowing God to work in our hearts, bringing spiritual renewal out of brokenness." — *Dr. Gary Benedict, President, Christian and Missionary Alliance*

Trade Paper ISBN 978-0-87508-873-0

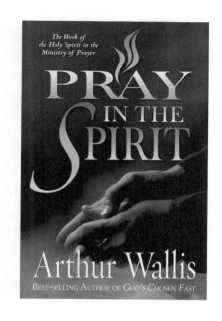

PRAY IN THE SPIRIT

ARTHUR WALLIS

How should I pray?
How can I prevail in prayer?

This book concentrates on these and other basic questions as well as on the ministry of the Holy Spirit in relation to prayer.

It investigates the deeper meaning of the apostolic command, "Pray in the Spirit."

Trade Paper ISBN 978-0-87508-574-6

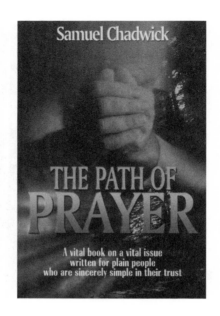

THE PATH OF PRAYER

SAMUEL CHADWICK

What is prayer and what are its functions? This helpful volume is based not on theory but experience, and is simply written so that everyone will be able to apply its principles.

Mass Market ISBN 978-0-87508-578-4

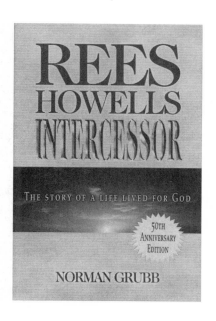

REES HOWELLS, INTERCESSOR

Norman Grubb

"A Welsh miner who became a spiritual giant. Here is the inspiring biography for all who would seek to do exploits for God. Well written in graphic language, it will inspire both old and young."

Trade Paper ISBN 978-0-87508-188-5